TESTIMONIALS

I was instantly mesmerized. Anne Shoshana Deakter's work has brought so much joy to my life, and it's brought me an inner peace that I can't describe. I'm so grateful to her and I highly recommend Anne Shoshana Deakter to everybody.

Michelle B.

Anne Shoshana Deakter is very inspirational. She helped me make a change in my life—by taking a look at where I was and where I wanted to be. She was very helpful in guiding me to that goal where I wanted to eventually find myself.

Robert S. Weinroth
Lawyer and Palm Beach County Commissioner

Anne Shoshana Deakter provides sound and practical advice for all real-life challenges. The incorporation of universal Torah principles provides an even greater depth to her sessions. I highly recommend Anne Shoshana Deakter if you are seeking a coach who goes beyond the textbook and touches your soul.

Miryam H.

Anne Shoshana Deakter is truly a blessing from up above. She continues to guide me on my path to success in my personal, financial, and spiritual journey. She is like someone who already knows the answers to my situation but who is helping me to figure it out in my own way and time. So many times we have worked on a specific area, and within a short time, amazing changes have occurred. I am so grateful for her in my life.

Howard H.

Anne Shoshana Deakter has taught many classes for the BRJE and I have only received positive feedback from the participants. She is excellent in making the material user friendly and ensuring that everyone always sees the relevance of this Universal Wisdom in their daily life.

Rabbi Josh Broide

Jewish Federation, South Palm Beach Florida/Boca Raton Jewish Experience (BRJE) and Outreach Rabbi of Boca Raton Synagogue

The surveys for your class "The Bigger the Challenge, the Greater the Fulfillment" showed the approval rate was 96 percent. Obviously, the attendees loved your class!

Anita H.

Program Director, 5th Annual Jewish Women's Study Day

YOU AREN'T HERE TO BE
GOOD
YOU ARE HERE TO BE
BETTER

# YOU AREN'T HERE TO BE
GOOD
YOU ARE HERE TO BE
BETTER

How to Reclaim Hope, Purpose, and Fulfillment
in a World Gone Crazy

ANNE SHOSHANA DEAKTER

© 2018 Anne Shoshana Deakter

All rights reserved. No part of this book may be reproduced or transmitted in any form or by any means, electronic or mechanical, including photocopying, recording, or by any information storage and retrieval system, except in the case of brief quotations embodied in critical articles and reviews, without prior written permission of the publisher.

Although the author and publisher have made every effort to ensure the accuracy and completeness of information contained in this book, we assume no responsibility for errors, inaccuracies, omissions, or any inconsistency herein.

Printed in the United States of America.
Library of Congress Control Number: 2018964140
ISBN: 978-1-949639-33-9

Cover Design: Carly Blake
Layout Design: Melanie Cloth

TABLE OF CONTENTS

TESTIMONIALS i

INTRODUCTION 1

CHAPTER 1 7

    You Aren't Here to Be Good;
    You Are Here to Be Better

CHAPTER 2 15

    If You're Not Moving Forward,
    You're Moving Backward

CHAPTER 3 23

    What Do You Want?

CHAPTER 4 33

    Don't Trust Your Five Senses

CHAPTER 5 43

    Is Your Life in the Green or in the Red?

CHAPTER 6 51

    Don't Tell Me What to Do

CHAPTER 7 .... **67**

    The Harder the Challenge, the Greater the Fulfillment

CHAPTER 8 .... **73**

    Stop the Voices in My Head

CHAPTER 9 .... **79**

    I'm Not Buying What You Have for Sale

CHAPTER 10 .... **95**

    Everything Happens for a Reason

CHAPTER 11 .... **101**

    As Long as You Are Breathing, You Will Be Fixing Something

CHAPTER 12 .... **105**

    One, Two, Three Strikes, You're Out

CHAPTER 13 .... **115**

    E.T. Phone Home

CHAPTER 14 .... **117**

    There Is Order in What Appears to Be All-Consuming Chaos

CHAPTER 15 .... **133**

Soul Pods

CHAPTER 16 .... **137**

Thank You and Keep in Touch

ACKNOWLEDGMENTS 139

ABOUT THE AUTHOR 143

CONNECT WITH ANNE SHOSHANA DEAKTER 145

INTRODUCTION

When I was thirty years old, I realized that there was more to life than the all-consuming pursuit of acquiring "things." Often it takes a wake-up call for most of us to make serious changes in our lives. We typically go through life refusing to see, self-medicating, or keeping so busy that we can't think or feel. My wake-up call was the early death of my beloved father and becoming a divorced single mom.

I was married for thirteen years and felt like I was going nowhere personally, professionally, spiritually, and emotionally. During that time, my father came for a visit and literally dropped dead in my house. I found him cold and blue on the bedroom floor. I had to tell my mom and then make arrangements to ship his body home. It was a nightmare. I felt adrift in my marriage and I didn't have a profession I loved to fall back on to fill the void.

I wasn't one of those people who always knew what they wanted to be. I had no idea what my purpose in life was. I had an inkling that I liked working with and teaching people, so I got my first degree in sociology. I tried to fill the gaping hole in my life with so many different things. I got my second degree in teaching, and continued on to pursue extensive graduate work at Florida Atlantic University's Department of Educational Leadership and Research Methodology.

I kept myself so busy, "unconscious," that I didn't have to think about how miserable my life was. It got to a point where running away and avoiding reality was no longer an option. I could no longer numb my pain. Looking back, I'm tremendously grateful to a friend who suggested that I go to a transformational workshop where I ended up meeting a group of like-minded people on a quest to better their lives.

I learned so much about myself there, how to be self-reliant, care for others, and I became a better person in the process. I also happened to find my life's purpose. Over the next two years, I rose in the ranks at the workshop and became a leader, coach, and mentor. I loved it.

I'll never forget the day of my graduation from the workshop. A stranger, a woman I had never met before, approached me and said, "You know what's next for you?" and I'm thinking to myself, *Yeah, sleep, and lots of it*. The past two years had been very strenuous on all fronts.

She told me to check out Kabbalah. I had no idea what she was talking about, but being the gracious person I am, there was no need to be rude, so I kindly nodded my head and moved on. A few weeks later, I attended the graduation of one of the students who I'd mentored and coached. To my surprise, the same woman approached me and asked me if I had looked into Kabbalah. Once more, I pretended to accept her recommendation and carried on with my life.

Shortly thereafter, I was at a client's house and she asked me if we could finish our business quickly as she was having a lecture that night and needed to set up the house. A little voice in my head prompted me to ask her who was coming to speak. She told me she was having a Rabbi come to her house to give a lecture on Kabbalah. Well, what can I say? I heard bells. It was my first "aha" moment! I asked her if I could come to the lecture, and that night I met the teacher with whom I have been studying Kabbalah and spirituality for the past twenty-four years.

I'm amazed when I look back and see where I started from and where I ended up. It's incredible to see how all the parts came together to create the fulfilled life I now live. In a million, trillion years, I never could have imagined my life turning out the way it did.

I am now remarried to a wonderful man, and together we had another son. The painful events of the past have de*finite*ly shaped and molded me into the person I am today. Did I enjoy the suffering that I went through? Heck no! But in hindsight, I can see that it had a purpose. It revealed to me my life's mission. It gave my life meaning and direction. Finally—what a great feeling!

I have come to realize that it's a rare person who can do this work alone. Most need support. I could never have gone through the many challenges that crossed my path without numerous mentors and friends by my side. These people were there to intervene when I was traveling down the wrong path, when I was too blind to see.

I am now able to share my journey and help others make their lives better as a leadership educator, concierge life coach, inspirational speaker, and author. For the past twenty-four years, I have also been a student and teacher of the ancient, immutable UNIVERSAL

WISDOM of the Old Testament, Mussar (Jewish self-help commentaries), and the Kabbalah (the ancient UNIVERSAL WISDOM that teaches you how to receive and manifest joy and fulfillment in all areas of your life). Throughout this book, I will use the term "UNIVERSAL WISDOM" to refer to the above sources.

I have created a program in which I fuse this ancient wisdom with my experience as a leadership educator. Using today's language, I provide user-friendly tools that make this complex Wisdom accessible, relatable, and easy to use and benefit from. Why? So that you, too, can be a better person. (And also because my students and private clients have been nudging me to put everything we do together into a book!)

At this time, I must be very clear that this book is for **ALL** of humanity to learn from. This is not a religious book, nor am I promoting one religion over another. There is no hidden religious agenda. I am generically sharing the wisdom of modern humanism brought to life by our common matriarch and patriarch, Sarah and Abraham. I sometimes use Hebrew words to help express universal concepts, as it is called the language of Creation, and many secrets that we need to know are contained within it.

As a life coach, the most common concern my clients share with me is that they don't have a clue as to what their life's purpose is, nor what their next steps should be. This appears to be a universal and demoralizing problem. So why are you here? You are here to enjoy an incredible journey of awe-inspiring transformation and fulfillment, to earn it on your own and be the creator of your own life. You are destined to be full of joy and bliss. Endless pain and suffering with no resolution was never supposed to play any part in your destiny.

Yes, life contains a series of never-ending challenges—some easier, and some harder than others. The good news is that there are tools you can use during difficult times that can help to shorten the challenge process and infuse it with mercy.

But you really have to want to do the work if you want to see any improvement. You have to know what motivates you. And if you don't know what motivates you, I've always found the following suggestion beneficial. Just keep moving and doing, with the understanding that putting one foot in front of the other eventually gets you where you need to go: to your next level of enlightenment and innovation. This type of "doing" is drastically different then keeping busy as a way to remain numb.

This brings to mind an expression my mother used to say, and it drove me crazy: "Yours is not to question why. Yours is just to do or die." It's only today that I begin to understand the depth and wisdom of it. During challenging times, when you are feeling down and don't know what is next, and you're in the space between leaving the old and discovering the new, the best plan is to keep moving. If you come to a full stop, the energy of death, end, will permeate all that you do. In those moments, no matter how often you ask, "Why is this challenge happening?" you are probably not going to get the answer you want. The only thing that will keep you sane is the "doing." The doing is different for everyone, but whatever you do, make it positive and productive. For some, it's going to the gym, cooking, taking up a new hobby, accepting a job that's below your pay grade, volunteering, etc. Just know that one thing leads to another until everything comes together to create a fulfilled whole. No effort is lost or wasted.

This journey would be so much easier if we were living in a loving, caring, and sharing world—but we are not. And that's why I wrote this book: to share with you the tools to reclaim hope, purpose, and fulfillment in a world gone crazy.

So ask yourself, do you really want your life to be great? Do you really want the world to be great? Do you really want to leave a bright legacy for future generations?

If you've answered yes to any of the above, that means you must *do* something about it. Living in a state of numb inertia is not going to fix the current negative, selfish, and "taking-focused" state of affairs. Yes, you have to run away from natural disasters (hurricanes, floods, wildfires, earthquakes, etc.), but if more people were focused on bettering themselves, one would hope that peace would reign and we wouldn't have to run away from human-created chaos, like school shootings and terrorist attacks.

The UNIVERSAL WISDOM is very clear that becoming a better person requires consistent effort. Did you know that at the end of your time here on this earth, you are going to be asked three questions when you stand in front of the Pearly Gates. One of these questions is did you set aside time each day to learn how to improve your life so that you can transform into the best version of yourself? (Babylonian Talmud, Shabbat 31a)

It is my pleasure to help you reacquaint yourself with the UNIVERSAL WISDOM that teaches that you are here to receive and create everything that is good and fulfilling.

So welcome, and let's get started.

CHAPTER 1

You Aren't Here to Be Good; You Are Here to Be Better

According to the UNIVERSAL WISDOM, the purpose of life is to transform into the self-actualized, fulfilled, abundant, and purpose-driven person you are destined to be.

Furthermore, it teaches that the world was created just for you—for your pleasure and enjoyment. (Babylonian Talmud, Sanhedrin 37a) You were never meant to live a life of ongoing chaos, pain, and suffering. What would happen if you put milk into the gas tank of a car? It would break down. The same thing happens to you if you put chaos, pain, and suffering into your body and soul: your life falls apart. All areas are affected; your relationships stop working, money stops flowing, you lose your patience with your kids, and you make lousy decisions. In general, you just lose it and it doesn't look or feel pretty.

What's done is done. We are all human and we've all "lost it" at some time or another. There's no need to rehash or belabor the point. Your becoming a better person, which means enhancements in all areas of your life (health, relationships, finances, purpose, etc.), is serious and exciting business. So let's focus on that. That's exactly what this book is about.

Every morning you get up, it's a new day, correct? It's not an old day; it's not a day that already occurred. Ideally, you are always involved in the new, in what's next. This need to learn and grow is written into your metaphysical DNA. We love new things—a new baby, new ideas, new technology, new philosophies, new toys, etc. There's just something so intoxicating about the new. I think this is because it gives us the illusion of starting all over again. It gives us hope for a better outcome, for a happier and more productive result. Why do I say "illusion"? You must be very careful not to fall into the trap of doing the same thing over and over again and expecting a different result, which is widely considered to be the definition of insanity. This means you must make it a firm priority to learn from your mistakes so you don't repeat them.

Unfortunately—and I don't mean to sound judgmental—a lot of people are afraid of the "new/next" and desperately hold on to their old ways of doing things.

My mentor loves to tell the following story: You're at the airport and the suitcases are going around the carousel in the Arrivals hall. It's possible for you to see inside each case. Inside each valise is a collection of all types and combinations of different challenges that can happen to someone, and you can choose which pack of troubles to take home with you. Logic would dictate that you would take home the suitcase with the easiest challenge to overcome. Human nature, however, shows us that we tend to stick with what is familiar, and we will gravitate to our own suitcase time and time again. It's easier to deal with the garbage we know than the garbage we don't know. It's not easy to let go.

So, please ask yourself, do you hold on to the old or do you make room for the new?

Learning the UNIVERSAL WISDOM may at first feel foreign, as it is literally like learning a new language. The new and unknown can at times feel uncomfortable. So please just sit in it and be with it.

Give it time and perspective, and eventually, slowly and surely, it will begin to feel like a well-worn and loved pair of jeans that you never want to part with. Getting comfortable with the uncomfortable is part of the transformative process. I know you can do it. It requires interpretation to make it user-friendly, practical, and relevant to today's life.

The UNIVERSAL WISDOM likes to use the language of Creation, Hebrew, to make sense of the Universe. *Gematria* is the process whereby a numerical value is assigned to each Hebrew letter, and the combination and rearrangement of specific letters into various words provides us with valuable information. The Hebrew letters of the word *peshat* (the acceptance of things at face value) can be rearranged to spell another Hebrew word, *tipesh,* which means stupid. The message conveyed is that you have to be stupid to accept things at face value.

You need to do your due diligence. Do you take everything at face value? Do you believe everything you are told? No, you apply intellect and reasoning. If you don't understand something, you brainstorm with people who have more knowledge than you, or you go directly to an expert in the field.

The same reasoning and logic can be applied to the learning of the UNIVERSAL WISDOM.

Intuitively, you know everything I am sharing with you. Don't take my word as law, however. I want you to test-drive everything you learn and then decide if the UNIVERSAL WISDOM is the right fit for you.

As a former horseback-riding champion, I can't help but use the following analogy: get ready for a wild and heady ride of eye-opening aha moments, ups and downs, and challenges to your existing way of thinking. I can't guarantee it; I can only share the results of thousands of my students and private clients, who tell me after learning this ancient, immutable UNIVERSAL WISDOM that they feel they have won a first-place ribbon. So, kudos to you! Whether you are new to this journey or have been on it for what seems like forever, we will walk the path of self-transformation and decode the UNIVERSAL WISDOM together.

Whenever I start a new course or give a lecture, I always ask the question, "Why are you here?" The most common answers are: "Curiosity." "I feel like I was led to you." "I feel like there is something missing." "I feel blocked." "I want to find my soul mate." "I want to be happy." "I want financial freedom." "I want to know what my life's purpose is." "I want to be healthy." And "I want to be the best version of me." These are great and noble answers, and it's really important that you understand where they are coming from.

The UNIVERSAL WISDOM teaches us that there are no coincidences, and everything happens for a reason. The fact that you're reading this book tells me that you're exactly where you need to be. It is the right time in your life to take on the project of bettering yourself. Your curiosity (or whatever factor led you to read this book) is a physical manifestation of your soul's desire to be noticed and nourished.

You have a body and a soul. For the most part, we know how to take care of the body. Your body lets you know when it needs to eat, sleep, go to the bathroom, fill its sexual needs, etc. The body is also a very effective "I want" machine. Its innate nature is to be selfish and "taking." It wants its toys and pleasures. There's nothing wrong with wanting the good things in life. The problem arises when you take whatever you want and do whatever you want, whenever you want, without thought or care for the pain and suffering you may cause yourself and others.

Taking care of the needs of the soul, however, is a completely different matter. In my professional experience, most people are not even aware of their soul's true desire. The UNIVERSAL WISDOM teaches that an essential component of living a fulfilled and abundant life is being able to nourish both body and soul in a balanced manner.

Why is it more difficult to identify what the soul needs, and so much easier to know what your body desires? First of all, the soul is not visible, so by default, it's a lot harder to connect with. The soul is all about expanded *Realms* of awareness, intuition, and intangible states of consciousness that cannot be experienced by the five senses.

But it does have a way of talking to you. Everything can be going great. Your relationship is good, your career is working, your life has meaning, but you still have an empty feeling inside, something is "off." That's your soul. The typical response to this cry for help is to fill this illusive void with distractions and materialism: a new car, designer clothes, overtime at work, one-night stands, etc. This might work temporarily, but eventually the pain of feeling that something's not working drives you to find answers.

That's why I'm not surprised when successful executives come to me for coaching under the guise of, "I need to make more money." Hey, whatever gets them through the door. But is that the real reason they are coming to me? No. Somehow they know that something (nourishing the soul) is missing; they just don't know how to express it.

Over the course of our time together, I get the privilege of watching them reacquaint themselves with their other half, their soul. I see them evolving into more balanced, happier, and fulfilled people. For many, I'm happy to report, there is a corresponding increase in income as well.

There is another reason why the soul is so quiet and hard to hear. I'm now going to introduce you to a very nasty energetic force that does not want you to have an intimate relationship with your soul. Actually, the reason for its existence is to do everything in its power to drive a wedge between you and your soul.

The UNIVERSAL WISDOM teaches us that there is also a dark force in the Universe. I have a hard time with the word "evil," so humor me as I work around it. This negative force has many names, you can call it whatever you want (Murphy, yetzer hara, evil inclination, the devil). I'm going to refer to it as the bad guy.

Do you remember those old TV cartoons in which a white angel sits on the right shoulder and the red devil sits on the left shoulder of a person in the middle of a moral dilemma? The two of them duke it out. The white angel whispers into the right ear words of encouragement for doing good deeds and making good choices. The red devil shouts into the left ear, "Are you kidding me?! Eat as much ice cream as you want, even if you are lactose intolerant. Steal from this one, take from that one, and just keep doing it!"

Yep, we are very familiar with these dudes. The UNIVERSAL WISDOM teaches we all have them as frequent guests in our psyche.

No, you are not crazy; these are the two voices talking in your head, and they've been with you since birth. Be on guard, however, when you hear the bad guy. Be hyper aware.

The bad guy always pipes up when you engage in activities that reveal positivity, growth, good energy, and happy feelings. It will do everything in its power to thwart your efforts at attaining enlightenment. Every time you pick up this book, the bad guy will do everything it can to make sure that something comes up to prevent you from reading. Oops, sorry; you are now officially on the bad guy's radar. My bad, ha-ha!

I want you to fight the bad guy's voice inside your head, telling you, "Why do you need this? You have to pay the bills, make money, take care of the kids, take care of your sick mother. You're too tired, too stressed! You just want to eat and climb into your jammies and check out. You don't have time for this nonsense! Everything is perfect just the way it is, so leave well enough alone. You don't have enough time in the day to breathe, let alone take on another project!"

The bad guy is a parasite and his job is to make sure that you are mired in one challenge after another, with no light at the end of the tunnel. Well, take a hike, bad guy; that's not going to happen on my watch. The bad guy is always going to be with you. The good news, however, is that you can learn how to gain mastery over the bad guy.

Transforming into the best version of yourself is your destiny and the UNIVERSAL WISDOM is going to light the way. Let's go!

QUICK REVIEW

You weren't put on this earth to be a good person; you were put on this earth to be *better*. Why do I say this? To set the scene for the definition of insanity, which is doing the same thing over and over again and expecting a different result. Wherever you are on this journey, there is an internal knowledge that it's got to get better than this. This is not the be all and end all. As long as you are living and breathing, there will always be a "next."

I talked about the comic representation of the white angel/red devil (bad guy) sitting on your shoulders. Whenever you're going to learn something that is going to release positive energy into the universe, the bad guy rears its ugly head and does everything in its power to make sure that you stay home, eat pizza, binge-watch TV, or take a bubble bath. You haven't colored your hair in three years, and tonight is the night you get the impulse to finally do it. The minute you decide to do anything that creates positive energy or "light," that's it; that's when Mr. bad guy comes out to play. So, keep reading, and fight your bad guy.

CHAPTER 2

If You're Not Moving Forward, You're Moving Backward

You know that expression, "In this world, nothing can be said to be certain except death and taxes"? Well, I'm going to add one more term to that exalted list: challenges. Challenges are a given, and they are not going to magically disappear, no matter how much you might wish they would.

What role do challenges play in your life? They help you grow. Challenges are opportunities that help you to overcome your limiting and damaging character traits, defined as the behaviors that create chaos, pain, and suffering. My students and private clients say, "Are you kidding me? That age-old, disgusting, iconic statement 'no pain, no gain'? Really? You want me to buy into this? You want me to accept as normal a world reality of overcoming one challenge after another?"

The good news is, with what you are about to learn, you will be able to mitigate the challenge so that the pain is lessened in severity and the time frame of the challenge is shortened. Now that's something to get excited about!

There are four different types of people I encounter when I teach and coach, and they are distinguished by how they react to challenges. I do an icebreaker exercise in which I tell a story. It sets the scene for my students to react in typically one of four ways.

I noticed that there is one specific type of person who gets the most out of life. This person recognizes that life is uncomfortable and full of adversity. This person also, however, creates a positive relationship with challenges that move him or her forward.

As you read the icebreaker exercise, identify which group you most closely relate to. There is no right or wrong. It's just an opportunity for you to think about how you react when you encounter new and challenging situations. The first step to making friends with challenges is developing awareness.

**

You haven't seen your best friend, who lives overseas, in over twenty years. A lot has changed during that time. In the beginning of this relationship, you sent and received letters using old airmail envelopes that folded over and contained no paper. Do you remember when it took a month to get that letter? It was the most exciting thing in the world, and when you wanted to open it up, you had to do it so carefully, because if you ripped it open too quickly, you were afraid you were going to rip through the words inside.

As the years went by, international phone service became more accessible, but still, when you spoke on the phone, it was super rushed because you knew the call was going to cost a small fortune.

Now that friend is finally coming to visit you. You can't wait. You get in your car and drive to the airport. You're so excited! Your heart is pounding. Your mouth is dry. This person owns a piece of your heart and has done so since the moment you met when you were just kids. You wonder, Will it feel awkward when we first lay eyes on each other after all this time?

All these anxious thoughts run through your head until time stands still, and in the distance, you see that person walking toward you. All the noise around you recedes. You start running toward each other. I want you to turn to the person on your right or left, and greet them as if they were that person you hadn't seen in twenty years.

* * *

Well, it's a real hoot for me to stand back and watch the activity, and over the years, there has emerged a *definite* pattern/reaction to this exercise. There are four common types of reactions I see:

FIRST TYPE:	I'm absolutely terrified. Is Anne Shoshana absolutely crazy? I am not doing this. I'm going into a corner to hide. I'm going to make myself as inconspicuous as possible.
SECOND TYPE:	I don't want to do this. I hate this. I am cringing inside. It's taking every ounce of my willpower to move forward, but I'll do the exercise because I don't want to look like a fool or like I'm not part of the group. I'll do it even though I am extremely uncomfortable.

THIRD TYPE:	I don't like it. I am uncomfortable, but I came here to learn. I came here for an experience, so even though it feels weird, I'm going to do it. I'm going to give it my all.
FOURTH TYPE:	I like people. I'm a hugger, so I'll just hug everyone.

How does knowing which type you are improve your life? It gives you an understanding of what you do when confronted with the next challenge. If you know how you are programmed, what your default setting is, then you can learn a better way of reacting to the challenge that will ensure that it is lessened in duration and suffering. Please identify which "Type" you are in the space provided below.

I am the _____ Type.

UNIVERSAL TRUTH #1:
Life is uncomfortable and full of challenges.

Trying to deny this is an exercise in futility. The UNIVERSAL WISDOM calls living in denial "dormita," the state of existence where we are like the living dead—sleepwalking aimlessly through life, going through the motions, like zombies. This takes place because the body and the soul are completely disconnected from each other.

The nature of the physical body is to be selfish and "taking," which is diametrically opposed to the soul, whose nature is more reflective of our Creator's, which is to be loving, caring, and sharing. The lack of connection between body and soul results in chaos. This chaos is uncomfortable and a major wake-up call. It's not a call we want to listen to, however. It's easier to deflect, take the path of least resistance, or numb the pain with all sorts of distractions.

The irony is that you can't run away from being uncomfortable. It follows you throughout your daily interactions. You're not comfortable when you visit the doctor, go to a job interview, discipline your kids, confront your significant other, stand up for yourself and set boundaries, etc.

Do you know how a diamond is formed? It's formed from coal, deep in the earth, and over time and under immense pressure, it becomes a diamond. If you want your best self to be beautiful, shiny, and sharing the light of many facets, then you must go through the same process. Pressure over time turns you into the best version of you, like a flawless diamond.

Taking the easy way out or the path of least resistance does not connect you to a sense of fulfillment or accomplishment. Rather, the quick and easy sense of satisfaction you get is quickly gone, leaving you with a bad taste in your mouth and a feeling of emptiness. You get a quick "hi," immediately followed by a "bye-bye."

This creates an endless, unfulfilling cycle whereby you are constantly looking for the next "high."

So, how do you change years of this negative belief system and negative programming? Enduring and long-lasting fulfillment is certainly not found in immediate gratification, materialism, and taking the easy way out.

It begins with accepting that life is full of challenges and "next," maybe even getting a little excited when a new and difficult test arises. OK, I get it; most people aren't happy when they realize they are facing a scary challenge. But just maybe you can put the brakes on your spiraling, panicking emotions, take a breath, and let the realization in that successfully overcoming any given challenge contributes to the transformation process, of turning you into the best version of yourself, the more fulfilled you. Now that's something to get excited about! Also, it feels freaking awesome when you can say, "I did it; I made it happen! I created light out of darkness."

Remember that icebreaker story I told you about meeting your best friend after having not seen each other in twenty years? There is no right or wrong type. But hopefully you're beginning to see that the Third Type, the person who thinks, *I'm definitely uncomfortable, but I'm going to do this icebreaker anyway,* is the person you want to become more like.

Why? Creating a healthy relationship with challenges will shorten their duration and lessen the severity of the pain they present. Challenges are a given. You will never be free of them, but you can discover how to learn and grow from them.

QUICK REVIEW:

I used the icebreaker exercise to explain that people react to challenges in four distinct ways, and I asked you to identify which category you belong to:

FIRST TYPE:	"I'm not going to do this, no matter what you say. I'm going into the corner to hide."
SECOND TYPE:	"I'm really uncomfortable with this, but everybody else is doing this, so I am going to do it, too, because I don't want look like a fool."

THIRD TYPE:	"I am also uncomfortable with what's going on, but I made a commitment to my being the best version of myself, so I'm giving it my all."
FOURTH TYPE:	"I'll hug anybody."

Based on years of experience doing this icebreaker activity, most people who attend my courses and read this book will fall into the third category.

Why? Because it is the right time in your life to take on yourself. You are ready to overcome whatever is in your way, even if you are uncomfortable doing so. This is the first step in getting to know yourself and the inner dialogue that runs you. I know—ew—self-introspection is almost as bad as confrontation, ha-ha!

Death, taxes, and challenges are part of life, and they are not going away.

If challenges are a given, it's essential that you know how you react when a challenge arises.

CHAPTER 3

What Do You Want?

So, yes, overcoming difficult challenges is a staple in your transformational diet. What a bitter pill to swallow! What will make it taste better? Working toward a goal, something that stimulates you and keeps you engaged and happy. With this in place, you are in a much better frame of mind to deal with challenges when they arise. What is this "goal"? It's working toward achieving your life's purpose, why you are here.

I've noticed in my private coaching practice and while giving lectures that people find answering this all-important question to be one of the hardest challenges they've faced. Most people don't know why they are here and what their purpose is.

It's time to seriously answer this major life question: What is your purpose; why are you here? You are here to create a life of hope, purpose, abundance, fulfillment, unity, and love. Chaos, pain, and suffering without resolution were never supposed to be part of the plan.

Simply put, your purpose is to correct yourself. The UNIVERSAL WISDOM calls it doing your *tikune* (a Hebrew word which means correction). You are born with a unique, beautiful purpose and potential. It's the negative character traits (and yes, we all have them) that get in the way of seeing your fulfilled potential manifested. We'll talk about how to discover what your *tikunim* (the plural of *tikune*) are, and fix them in chapter 11.

So, to help you gain some clarity, to help you answer the age-old question, "What is your purpose?" I'll share with you an exercise that I do in my lectures that gives the participants a clear idea of what humanity ultimately wants, which translates into what the soul ultimately wants.

I have two volunteers come up to the board and I ask the following question: "What do you want?" I ask the class to shout out their answers, and the volunteers write everyone's answers on the board. It's fast and furious, funny and zany.

These are the answers that are typically given in every class I have ever taught. It never changes; it rarely varies.

Peace. Calm. Joy. Love. Health. Happiness. Satisfaction. Kindness. Balance. Stimulation. Unity. Friendship. Self-awareness. Prosperity. Success. Self-expression. Play. Laughter. Soul mates. Creativity. Inspiration. Tranquility. Wisdom. Pleasure. Clarity. Make a difference. To share. Purpose. To serve. Curiosity. Transformation. Excitement. Motivation. Exhilaration. Serenity. Adventure. Spirituality. Compassion. Connection to a Higher Power. Being in the moment. Family. Freedom. Enlightenment.

If I've missed any, which I'm sure I have, write them down here:

_____

_____

_____

Why do I do this exercise? One of the major tools of self-transformation is self-awareness. If you don't know what you want, how can you work toward achieving anything? Without a reason to live, without purpose, focus, and direction, life can feel empty. So this exercise is the first step in bringing to light what it is you truly want, what your soul truly wants.

So, back to the list. There is an interesting phenomenon that often occurs. There is one word that is consistently left off the list: passion. It's almost as if the expectation of living a life of passion has been beaten out of us. I truly hope that after you have finished reading this book, passion will once more be a mainstay in your life.

After compiling the answers on the board, I then ask the volunteers to read the list out loud. I ask them to look at the list and tell me what all of these terms have in common. Do you know what it is?

All of these words are intangible. Can you bottle *motivation* and put it on your nightstand? Can you take *wisdom* and put it in an envelope and mail it to somebody? Can you take *self-awareness*, package it, and sell it in the mall?

But what's wrong with you guys? How come you didn't tell me you wanted a new Mercedes? What about the designer handbags? The new house? Where is the new technology: Alexa, iPhone, Mac, etc.? Where are all the toys?

Invariably a student will yell out, "That's not true; money is tangible!" Really? So, what do you want to do with the money?

Do you actually want to touch it, play with it, take a bath in it? NO! You want what the money can buy, which is the most precious commodity of all: freedom.

Ultimately, money allows you the illusion of having control over your life. You want to be free to do what you want, when you want, and how you want. How does the song go? *Don't tell me what to do; don't tell me what to say.* We hate it when anyone tries to control us.

I've done this exercise with thousands of people and they all answer the same. No one ever mentions the toys. Why? What you really want is to transform into the best version of yourself in this lifetime—to earn the joy and fulfillment on your own and be the creator of your own life. **This is the true desire of the soul.**

When I realized that Hurricane Irma was going to be a Category 5, having already lived through Andrew, I decided immediately that we were leaving because there was no way I was going through that again. I packed my car, taking with me the things that mattered most to me: my children, my mother, my Torah (an actual scroll of the Five Books of Moses), my dog, our passports, and some clothes. And then I took off. Was there going to be anything to come back to? Did I even care? Not really. It was just stuff, toys.

As a matter of fact, two days before we left, we were supposed to take ownership of a car we had just leased. So I called the leasing agent and I told her to cancel it. When she asked why, I replied, "Because it's going to sit in the driveway during the hurricane and could possibly be destroyed. It's just a thing, a toy." I didn't care. It could always be replaced, while our lives could not.

This list of words . . .

Peace. Calm. Joy. Love. Health. Happiness. Satisfaction. Kindness.

Balance. Stimulation. Unity. Friendship. Self-awareness. Prosperity. Success. Self-expression. Play. Laughter. Soul mates. Creativity. Inspiration. Tranquility. Wisdom. Pleasure. Clarity. Make a difference. To share. Purpose. To serve. Curiosity. Transformation. Excitement. Motivation. Exhilaration. Serenity. Adventure. Spirituality. Compassion. Connection to a Higher Power. Being in the moment. Family. Freedom. Enlightenment.

. . . represents a state of consciousness called Light & Fulfillment, and a place that the UNIVERSAL WISDOM refers to as the *Infinite Realm*—the home of the soul and the Higher Power/God/Universal Light Force.

As beings in a physical body where things have a beginning and an end, we live in the *Finite Realm*, which also happens to be the world of challenges.

Together we're going to learn how to **bridge** to the *Infinite Realm*. According to the UNIVERSAL WISDOM, this is the real work of self-transformation. This is corroborated by the thousands of students who have gone before you and voiced their souls' truest desire: to connect to Light & Fulfillment.

UNIVERSAL TRUTH #2
All we want in life is to be full of Light & Fulfillment.

All of humanity wants to be full of "light." My students tell me, "I'm not sure I even know what that feels like. I've been living in survival mode for so long. I can't even relate to what I'm hearing." Then with much skepticism, I hear, "What you are talking about doesn't even exist. It's a fairytale, like 'Cinderella.'"

So, maybe at this juncture I need to remind you what being full of "light" feels like.

How do you feel when you fall in love? How do you feel when you are on an adventure, checking off an item on your bucket list? How did you feel after giving birth or after meeting your first grandchild? How do you feel after closing a major business deal? How do you feel after you've accomplished a major life goal? How do you feel when you are healed from a major illness?

Usually, you feel like you're going to explode from happiness. You are so full of "light," that you will simply burst if you can't share the feeling. You want to scream from the rooftops, sharing your joy with everyone. When we see a great movie, eat at an amazing restaurant, receive great news, we tend to immediately reach for the phone or post on social media, "OMG, it was amazing! You have to experience it!" When you are living your life's purpose, a natural extension of that is that you are compelled to share.

I'm going to tell you a story about one of my students and how she discovered what her life's purpose is. Hopefully, it will get you thinking in the right direction.

***

One day, I asked my advanced class to identify their life's purpose. They had such a hard time answering. I have an amazing student. She is a Holocaust survivor and she is asked to go on the March of the Living most years (an experiential trip that teenagers and adults take to visit concentration camps and learn about the Holocaust). She's in her late seventies, and she goes as a leader, which is very emotionally taxing and draining. It's cold and she's tired and it's a very rough trip in many ways: physically, emotionally, and spiritually.

In my naïveté, I was so sure that when she was asked what her life's purpose was, she would tell me teaching about the Holocaust and going on the March of the Living. So I sat there, very certain that this was what she was going to say. I was stunned when she told me that her life's purpose was to take care of her husband and to make his dinner every night.

I said, "Really, let me ask you a question: 'Do you get really excited to cook his dinner every night; are you on fire with passion and energy and excitement when going to the supermarket to buy the food?'"

She looked at me and said, "I feel bad to say it, but no."

So, I asked her, "What makes you feel like that: so on fire and excited that you don't sleep, and you have to share, you have to love, you have to care, have to give?"

I'm leading her at this point, obviously.

She pauses for a second.

"Oh, that's easy; when I go on the March of the Living, I feel exactly like that. I don't sleep for days. I barely eat and I'm totally in service. That's my life's purpose!" she says stunned and surprised. "That's what juices me. That's what makes me feel alive. I never thought of it that way. I just thought, *I'm a Holocaust survivor; this is what I should be doing.*"

She never took the trip for granted again. After her next trip, she told me how much her whole perspective of the trip had changed. She now realizes what an incredible contribution she is to the world and how great that makes her feel.

She said, "I'm in my seventies and I feel like a spring chicken! How cool is that?"

***

So how is it possible that something so difficult physically, spiritually, and emotionally brings her so much joy that she continues to do it year after year?

Don't you usually give up when something is very hard and intense? But what if the reward was worth all the effort because it brought you so much fulfillment? You felt so alive! The colors were brighter, all the dots were connected, things made sense, you had abundant energy, you couldn't wait to get up in the morning, and you had purpose. Then, yes, absolutely, without question, you would continue to do it. This is what it means to live your life's purpose and be full of "light."

This sense of fullness, being full of "light," is a spiritual/intangible and sacred experience. It's not physical, because it can't be bottled and it cannot be experienced with the five senses.

Again, we live in two realities: the physical/*Finite Realm* and the spiritual/*Infinite Realm*. From now, on I will use the term *Finite Realm* when referring to physical reality (where selfishness, taking, immediate gratification, materialism, and the energy of "end" prevails), and the term *Infinite Realm* when referring to the spiritual reality (home of the soul, Light & Fulfillment, and the Higher Power/God/Universal Light Force).

This "light" is your sacred destiny, but you don't know yet the universal rules, tools, and language that will allow you to access this "light." We get a clue that this is true from the Hebrew word *Kabbalah* (one of the ancient sources of the UNIVERSAL WISDOM). The infinitive of the word *Kabbalah* is *le-kabel* which means, "to receive."

Wow! What are you supposed to be receiving, you may ask? Light & Fulfillment. Our collective life's purpose is to receive fulfillment in all areas of our lives. Hmmmm, Light & Fulfillment exists in the *Infinite Realm* and we live in the *Finite Realm*. OK, I hear you loud and clear. You want to know how to get to the *Infinite Realm*, and fast. Follow me!

QUICK REVIEW:

I shared with you an exercise that I do in my lectures where volunteers come to the board and write down the answers to the question, "What do you want?" All of the answers have something in common. What is it? They are all intangible. You can't take happiness and put it in a bottle. You can't take freedom and put it on your bedside table and admire it. You can't cuddle at night with spontaneity.

So what is it that humanity ultimately wants?

UNIVERSAL TRUTH #2
All we want in is to be full of Light & Fulfillment.

Being full of "light" is enduring and long lasting. Being full of food is temporary. We exist in two realities: the *Finite Realm* (physical world) ruled by the basic desires of the physical body, and the *Infinite Realm* (spiritual/intangible world), the home of the soul and the Higher Power/God/Universal Light Force. Light & Fulfillment make their home in the *Infinite Realm*.

CHAPTER 4

Don't Trust Your Five Senses

In the *Finite Realm,* physicality rules 24/7—so much so, that the bad guy keeps you distracted by looking for the next "high" in the crazy and pointless pursuit of more, bigger, and better. This is how the bad guy has conspired for millennia to keep you in the dark.

Why when thousands of students were asked, "What do you want?," did not one of them say they wanted a Mercedes? No one said they wanted a new house. No one said they wanted a complete body makeover. Why wasn't the body yelling out its desire for expensive toys, advanced social standing, and physical gratification in its many forms?

Because what humanity ultimately wants, what the soul wants, is to be full of Light & Fulfillment in an enduring and long-lasting way. So we have a big challenge. We have to figure out how to **bridge** the gap between the physical (*Finite Realm*) and the spiritual (*Infinite Realm*) worlds, because everything we truly want (Light & Fulfillment) can only be found in the *Infinite Realm*.

I repeat: I am not saying you have to give up your toys to connect to the *Infinite Realm*. You can have all the toys you want. You can have the Mercedes, the house, the yacht, technology, designer clothes, etc.

If you willingly adopt the tools outlined in this book, you can be a master in both the *Finite* and *Infinite Realms*. There is no contradiction. You must have fun, money, vacations, and all the good things in life. Sarah and Abraham (of the Old Testament), the mother and father of modern humanism, were extremely wealthy and extremely wise. They were the masters of loving, caring, and sharing. Because of this, they were able to build a magnificent **bridge** to the *Infinite Realm,* and they were blessed with health, wealth, longevity, children, and a legacy that still lives on today.

The world is structured in a very specific way. Each *Realm* has its own **emotions/feelings** and **language**. Once you know what they are, it will be so easy for you to identify which *Realm* is dominant at any given moment in time.

Let's begin by defining the makeup of each of the *Realms*. To know which *Realm* is in control at any given moment, it is imperative that you become a pro at monitoring your inner dialogue. You have to be self-aware and listen to your self-talk. We tend to talk to ourselves a lot, even though we are not conscious of it. In particular, the GOOD GUY (voice of the white angel) and bad guy (voice of the red devil) talk to us nonstop. It's imperative that you weed through the noise so you can identify who is talking to you: GOOD GUY or bad guy.

The **language** of the *Finite Realm* sounds like this: "I don't want and I don't like (judgment). I don't want to get up in the morning and I don't want to see this person and I don't want this and I don't like that."

Are you even aware of when you are embroiled in a negative internal dialogue? It is so hard to identify because it has become second nature, automatic pilot, an accepted default setting.

The **emotions/feelings** that represent the *Finite Realm* are: sad, mad, depressed, jealousy, hopeless, lack, self-doubt, ego, fear, victim consciousness, and judgment. It sounds like, "You're not good enough and you're never going to make something of yourself. It's not fair! Why can she make it and I can't? He did it to me; it's not my fault! I don't like it. It's never going to work. I'm better than you. I'm afraid." Can you guess which cartoon character rules this *Realm*? You got it: the bad guy, the little red devil that sits on your left shoulder whispering all this negativity into your ear.

I have a friend who is an immigration attorney, and she told me that a potential client called her. After the call, she had a gut feeling that this was not going to be a good match, and yet she still accepted him as a client. Why didn't she listen to her intuition, her GOOD GUY?

What could possibly entice us to go against our morals, ethics, values, and good sense? What else? The bad guy. There was a lot of money to be made from the deal. She told me how the client then started talking down to her, demeaning her, and disrespecting her time, so she fired him.

She said, "I could've saved myself a lot of pain and suffering if I would have listened the first time I heard the little whisper, the voice of the GOOD GUY say, 'Why are you allowing this person to treat you like this?'" Selling yourself out for money, recognition, acknowledgement, etc. has nothing to do with the "light."

As I continue to explain how the universe is structured, I will continue to fill in the diagram called **Bridges to Light & Fulfillment** to give you a bird's-eye view of this amazing system. Once you understand it, internalize it, and work with it, this will become your greatest tool on your journey to a better you.

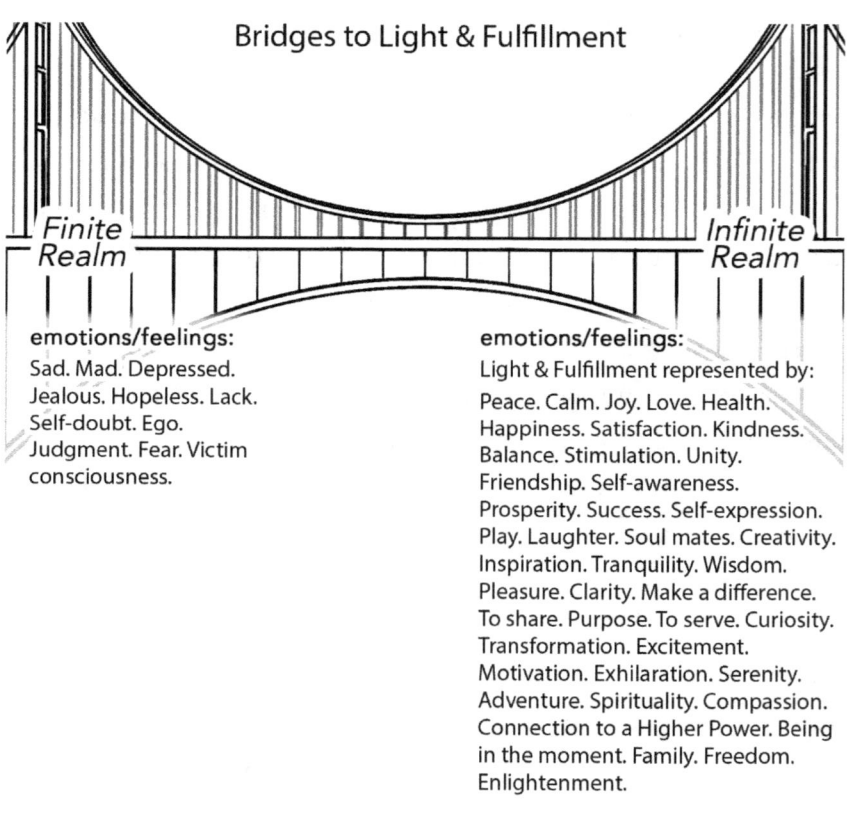

Bridges to Light & Fulfillment

Finite Realm

emotions/feelings:
Sad. Mad. Depressed. Jealous. Hopeless. Lack. Self-doubt. Ego. Judgment. Fear. Victim consciousness.

Infinite Realm

emotions/feelings:
Light & Fulfillment represented by:
Peace. Calm. Joy. Love. Health. Happiness. Satisfaction. Kindness. Balance. Stimulation. Unity. Friendship. Self-awareness. Prosperity. Success. Self-expression. Play. Laughter. Soul mates. Creativity. Inspiration. Tranquility. Wisdom. Pleasure. Clarity. Make a difference. To share. Purpose. To serve. Curiosity. Transformation. Excitement. Motivation. Exhilaration. Serenity. Adventure. Spirituality. Compassion. Connection to a Higher Power. Being in the moment. Family. Freedom. Enlightenment.

language:
I want...
I don't like...
I don't want...

language:

body ruled by: <u>bad guy</u>

soul ruled by: <u>GOOD GUY</u>

YOU AREN'T HERE TO BE GOOD, YOU ARE HERE TO BE BETTER

I want to prove to you that when you live life as an "*I want machine*," caring only about your own selfish needs and desires, you don't make the best choices in life. The evidence (the chaos and suffering that results from these choices) points to the facts that these choices keep you mired in the *Finite Realm*. One bad choice leads to another bad choice until all of a sudden, you are up to your neck in alligators and you can't see the forest for the trees.

So, how am I going to prove this to you?

I do the following exercise in my seminars, and I would now like to do it with you.

You are going to read a very famous teaser/optical illusion called "Alzheimer's Eye Test" and it's the most . . . well . . . you're about to find out! Follow these instructions:

- Read it one time only.
- Write down how many Fs you counted in the space provided.
- DO NOT write on the text.
- Read for no longer than ten seconds.

Start Now.

FINISHED FILES ARE THE RESULT OF YEARS OF SCIENTIFIC STUDY COMBINED WITH THE EXPERIENCE OF YEARS ...

How many letter Fs did you see? _____

I give my students ten seconds to count the Fs. Then I ask them to call out how many Fs they counted. After a few seconds, the seminar participants realize that something strange is going on. Why are so many different numbers being called out? So I tell them to read it once more, with the same instructions.

**FINISHED FILES ARE THE RE-
SULT OF YEARS OF SCIENTI-
FIC STUDY COMBINED WITH
THE EXPERIENCE OF YEARS …**

How many letter Fs did you see? _____

Did you count the same number of Fs the second time around, or did you get a different number?

At this point in the seminar, everybody is very confused and has no idea what's going on, so I read the text aloud and we count how many Fs there really are. I'm going to underline the text. Count with me.

**<u>F</u>INISHED <u>F</u>ILES ARE THE RE-
SULT O<u>F</u> YEARS O<u>F</u> SCIENTI-
<u>F</u>IC STUDY COMBINED WITH
THE EXPERIENCE O<u>F</u> YEARS …**

There are six Fs. Did any of you get that number the first or second time you read it? My experience with thousands of seminar participants guides me to state that most of you did not. Why? And what am I trying to teach you with this exercise?

UNIVERSAL TRUTH #3
Don't trust the five senses to interpret the Universe; you don't see the bigger picture. You don't see the whole truth.

That's really scary because, do you realize that you make life-altering decisions based on a small fraction of information available to you through your five senses (sight, hearing, touch, smell, and taste)? The five senses are residents of the *Finite Realm*, so already you should be getting a sense of their limited nature.

We live in a world where so many things are hidden from the naked eye, like microwaves, electric currents, radio waves, etc. Does this mean that they don't exist? There is so much you do not see. I liken this experience to the *Titanic*. The *Titanic* didn't have lifesaving sonar that could see below the waves, and neither do you have lifesaving "sonar" that sees into the *Infinite Realm*, the domain of all things good, empowering, and protective (Light & Fulfillment).

It comes as no surprise, however, that we are most adept at maneuvering through the *Finite Realm*. Why? Because in this world, we have something tangible to fall back on: the five senses. This is a world of, "I need to see it to believe it." So if it smells bad, it is bad. If it looks big, it is big. If it looks small, it's small. No brainer.

But when it comes to the really important things, life-altering decisions are made with only a small percentage of the facts available, which are gleaned from the *Finite Realm*.

Let's take an iceberg for example. Are you aware of the fact that the part of the iceberg that is actually visible to the naked eye is only around 10 percent? Approximately 90 percent is hidden from view. If you rely solely on your five senses for intel, you will be missing a huge chunk of info necessary to make balanced decisions—decisions that will significantly reduce the amount of suffering, pain, and chaos in your life.

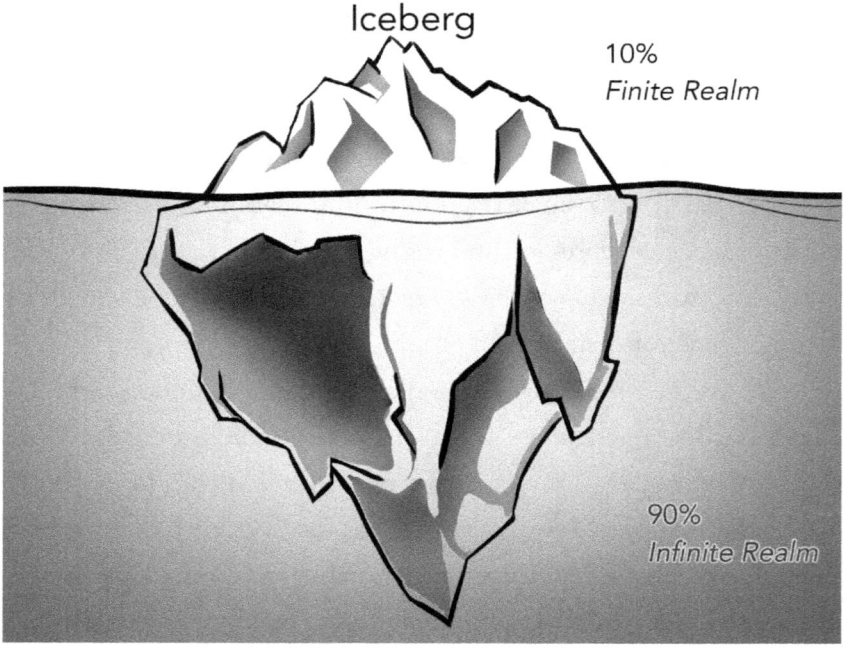

My students tell me emphatically that they want what's concealed in the *Infinite Realm,* and I know you want it too. Yes, life is very limited when you live in the 10 percent (*Finite Realm*) because it doesn't allow you to live your full potential. Now you understand why you sometimes feel blocked and blind. Why you don't see the full picture, and why intuitively you are hesitant to make decisions, is because you don't have confidence that you possess enough information to make the right choice.

The opposite is true when you master how to **bridge** to the *Infinite Realm*. You will have an immeasurable advantage that will enhance your life in all ways: better financial opportunities, deep and committed relationships, great health, self-actualization, and the joy of living your life's purpose.

QUICK REVIEW:

I introduced you to the F test to prove that you cannot trust your senses to connect you to the *Infinite Realm*. There are so many things around you that cannot be experienced with the five senses, like microwaves, electric currents, radio waves, etc. So if you can't trust your five senses, what *can* you trust? We've been programmed since birth to only believe what our eyes can see.

I used the *Titanic* as an example. When an iceberg/challenge comes along, you usually smash into it because you don't have lifesaving "sonar" to guide you. The only portion of the iceberg that you see is the ~10 percent that is above the surface; you don't see the ~90 percent that is below it. Major life decisions are made based on only 10 percent of the information available to you. So, where is the other 90 percent of the information? That information is in the *Infinite Realm*.

CHAPTER 5

Is Your Life in the Green or in the Red?

OK, enough already, I get it; you want to know how to make a **bridge** to the *Infinite Realm*. You want to start living a life of Light & Fulfillment now! This is where the fun begins. This is where you really start to get to know yourself and begin feeding your soul.

Becoming self-aware and cognizant of what you want and what you tell yourself (positive and negative) are crucial elements in becoming a master **bridge** maker. Do you talk nicely to yourself ("You look good today. You're going to knock their socks off with your presentation!")? Or do you doubt yourself and worry that the day is going to be a total failure? Self-awareness is the first step. Let's take it together.

There are six specific tools/**bridges** I will focus on to transport you to the *Infinite Realm* (there are many more, but these are the basics):

> **Bridge #1:** Monitor your internal dialogue.
>
> **Bridge #2**: I am a loving, caring, sharing creator.
>
> **Bridge #3:** I made it happen; I am cause.
>
> **Bridge #4:** 4-Step Creator Process.
>
> **Bridge #5:** Do your *tikune*.
>
> **Bridge #6:** I take so I can share.

Bridge #1: Monitor your internal dialogue.

Look at your life the way you would a business. At the end of the day, you take the cash out of the register, count it, and see how you did. Hopefully you're in the green and not in the red. You'll do this again at the end of the month, and at the end of the year, closely monitoring your success or failure. If month after month, year after year, you're continually losing money, then hopefully you would come to the realization that this business isn't working and you can either close the business, get a job, start a new company, or change the way you're doing business.

The UNIVERSAL WISDOM strongly urges you to look at your life the same way. At the end of the day, do a personal accounting. Before you go to bed at night, ask yourself, "Was this a day worth living? Did I move forward or did I move backward? Did I come out in the green or did I come out in the red?"

This is what it means to monitor your internal dialogue (**Bridge #1**). If you don't realize what's going on today, how will you know where to improve tomorrow? Living in the dark, in denial, you will continue to make the same mistakes and perpetuate your fixed existence in the *Finite Realm*, the home of pain, misery, and suffering. This form of personal introspection is very hard. No one wants to do it; no one likes to look within and see the garbage and dirt.

We are all very good at distractions: going shopping, dining out, working overtime, etc. Once you understand and accept that true self-introspection is a **bridge** to the *Infinite Realm*, hopefully you will jump at the opportunity to run across it. It's your choice. You have free will.

This means you stop and recognize when you are choosing a thought or action that leads you down the pain, suffering, and chaos path. Monitor your inner dialogue. If you hear yourself saying, "I don't want, I want, I don't like" (**language** of the *Finite Realm*), recognize this negative self-talk. You will then know that you are operating from the *Finite Realm*. Once you become cognizant of this, you can quickly reframe things and begin the process of building a **bridge** to the *Infinite Realm*.

Bridge #2: I am a loving, caring, sharing creator.

A loving, caring, sharing creator is a person who gives others the benefit of the doubt, sees the good in others, looks for win-win solutions, thinks before he speaks negatively, seeks to empower others, treats himself and others with human dignity, and takes personal responsibility.

Whoa! I get it; that's a tall order. So let's apply the Kiss Principle (keep it simple, stupid).

I want you to try something. Every time you hear yourself telling yourself anything negative (*Finite Realm* **language**): "I'm not good enough. I don't like this one. He's not doing it right. I'm mad. I'm sad. I am depressed. I'm jealous. I'm afraid," I want you to catch yourself. Stop the voice in your head (it's the bad guy at it again) and say instead, "I am a loving, caring, sharing creator" (*Infinite Realm* **language**).

You can say it all day long, a million times a day. You will be amazed how it shifts you from *Finite* **emotions/feelings** into *Infinite* **emotions/feelings** (look at the **Bridges to Light & Fulfillment** diagram if you need to be reminded). Changing years of negative self-talk takes time, and I'm not suggesting that this affirmation is going to undo the damage accumulated over a lifetime. This is just the beginning. It's where I have all my clients start. It takes effort and time to build *Infinite* muscles.

This is so powerful. Why? Because "I am" is *Infinite* **language**. It is the response God gave to Moses at the burning bush when Moses asked Him His name, and God replied, "I am who I am." (Bible, Exodus 3:14)

Basically, God was telling Moses, *I come from the Infinite Realm and that is where you're going to get the help, strength, confidence, wisdom, and perseverance you need to lead the Israelites out of bondage.* We, too, are in bondage. To what? To our bad guy and the selfish, taking part of our nature.

A relevant question to ask at this time is: Is there such a thing as how much "light" a person/soul can hold? Yep, souls come in all sizes; not one soul fits all. The most important thing for you to know about your soul—uh-oh, I feel another Universal Truth coming on …

UNIVERSAL TRUTH #4
The size of the soul is determined by how much you **desire** Light & Fulfillment.

The UNIVERSAL WISDOM shares that we are all born with different-sized souls. A soul can be compared to a vessel. Some containers can hold a lot of stuff, and some can hold only a small amount. Is it possible to expand your soul/vessel? Absolutely. As you grow and transform, so too does the size of your soul. It is able to hold more and more "light." This is a good thing. Every time you build and cross the **bridge** to the *Infinite Realm,* you are by default expanding your vessel. How great your desire is for the "light" will determine whether you have an expanding vessel or shrinking vessel.

A bigger vessel doesn't mean that you are a better person. So don't assign that type of judgment to this. The bottom line is for you to be the best version of you. And as long as you are moving forward and not moving backward, you're doing great. Everyone moves at his or her own pace. It is not a race.

Bridges to Light & Fulfillment

Bridge:

#1: Monitor your internal dialogue.

#2: I am a loving, caring, sharing creator.

#3:

#4:

#5:

#6:

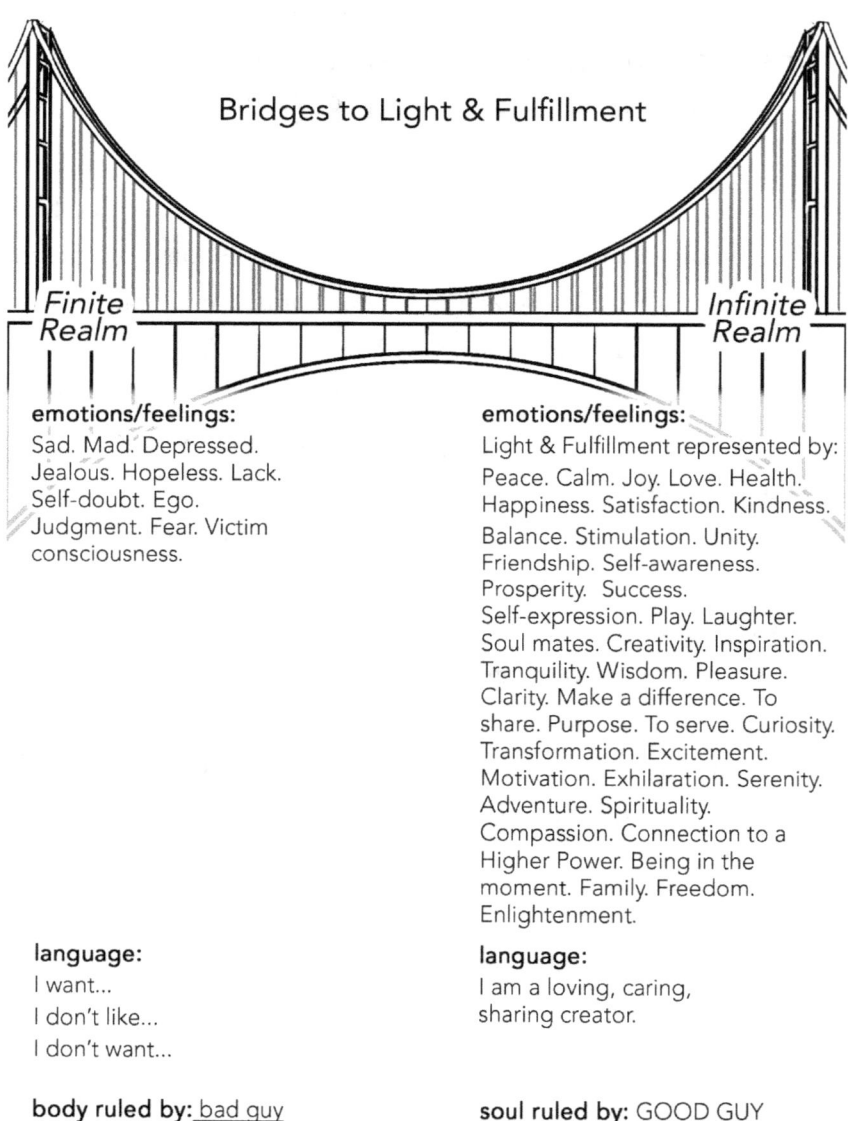

Bridges to Light & Fulfillment

Finite Realm

emotions/feelings:
Sad. Mad. Depressed. Jealous. Hopeless. Lack. Self-doubt. Ego. Judgment. Fear. Victim consciousness.

language:
I want...
I don't like...
I don't want...

body ruled by: <u>bad guy</u>
-five senses
-shrinking vessel

Infinite Realm

emotions/feelings:
Light & Fulfillment represented by: Peace. Calm. Joy. Love. Health. Happiness. Satisfaction. Kindness. Balance. Stimulation. Unity. Friendship. Self-awareness. Prosperity. Success. Self-expression. Play. Laughter. Soul mates. Creativity. Inspiration. Tranquility. Wisdom. Pleasure. Clarity. Make a difference. To share. Purpose. To serve. Curiosity. Transformation. Excitement. Motivation. Exhilaration. Serenity. Adventure. Spirituality. Compassion. Connection to a Higher Power. Being in the moment. Family. Freedom. Enlightenment.

language:
I am a loving, caring, sharing creator.

soul ruled by: <u>GOOD GUY</u>
-intuition
-expanding soul

Back to the business analogy. Once you learn to efficiently **bridge** to the *Infinite Realm*, you will see the positive change in your efforts at self-transformation. You can say that today you were a little happier than yesterday. There is justification for the business of your life to go on. And if this trend continues, it creates feelings of excitement, hope, purpose, and anticipation for a "light"-filled tomorrow.

Does this sound familiar? Where have you heard these words before? Oh yeah, under the *Infinite Realm* column in the **Bridges to Light & Fulfillment** diagram. You actually start looking forward to tomorrow, next month, next year, and the rest of your life. Wow! Again, Universal Truth #2: All we want is to be full of Light & Fulfillment.

QUICK REVIEW:

Bridge #1: Monitor your inner dialogue. Most of humanity is so unconscious that they are not even aware of these negative conversations playing over and over in their minds. Doing this internal work is not pleasant because it's not fun to look inside at the garbage accumulated by years of making limited choices and letting the bad guy get to you. You now know better. You must stop and catch yourself; identify the **language** and **feelings** of the *Finite Realm*. That's step number one.

The second you identify *Finite* **language** and **feelings**, replace them immediately with the mantra of **Bridge #2**: I am a loving, caring, sharing creator. Why? The Universal Life Force is *Infinite*, and we are *Finite* beings.

The only way to **bridge** to the *Infinite Realm* is by emulating the Godlike characteristics of loving, caring, sharing, and creating. This is God talk, and it has an affinity with the *Infinite Realm*, the place of Light & Fulfillment. The minute you say, "I am," you create a **bridge** to the *Infinite Realm*. You will probably find yourself saying this phrase more times a day than you can count.

CHAPTER 6

Don't Tell Me What to Do

Let's take a moment and talk specifically about the attribute of creator (*Infinite Realm* **language**). Creating has its own set of spiritual rules. Not all creations contribute to the building of a **bridge** to the *Infinite Realm*. The need to create and be the cause of all things, both good and bad in our life, is a need as old as time. Why? Because we inherited the "creating" DNA from the Higher Power in the *Infinite Realm*. There is no greater feeling than being able to say, "I did it; I made it happen."

We have a little problem. As physical beings, we have a natural affinity with the physical world.

How do we access this all important "creator" gene when it's embedded in a *Realm* that we don't have an affinity for? How do we connect to a reality with which we are not compatible?

The best way I can explain the *Infinite Realm* is in the following way: The *Infinite Realm* is the home of the Higher Power/God/Universal Life Force (use whatever name you can relate to). There is no limit to what the Higher Power can do, and it is not possible to define it or put it in a box. The only things you can relate to are some of the attributes that personify this *Realm* and its "King."

You are already familiar with some of the *Infinite Realm's* characteristics. What are they? The Universal Life Force is loving, caring, sharing, and creating. Therefore, if you want to build a **bridge** to this *Realm*, the home of Light & Fulfillment, then I highly suggest you focus on emulating these *Infinite* characteristics.

I'll set the scene for **Bridge #3** (I made it happen; I am cause.) with a story that my mentor loves to tell.

***

A young woman just graduated Harvard Business School with honors. She wanted to get a job at the company of her choice. She sent out her CV, and lo and behold, she got the job. She was really ambitious and wanted to go to the top, so the first year, she went the extra mile and worked like a dog. A year went by, and she was called to the boss's office. He told her that the board of directors was very impressed with her hard work and wanted to promote her.

How did she feel? Great! Full of "light." "I made it! I did it on my own! I earned it!" She was elated and full to bursting. She was so full of "light" because she had accomplished something so amazing. If she didn't share the good news with someone soon, she felt she would pop. She left the office flying high.

Suddenly, she remembered that she forgot to tell her boss an amazing idea she had to improve one of their accounts, so she went back to his office. He was already on the phone and had his back to her, so, being polite, she didn't make a sound. While waiting patiently for a short while, she realized that her boss was on the phone with her father. The conversation she overheard went like this:

"Hey, Bob, I did exactly what you asked me to do. Yeah, I gave her the corner office. Yep, she has the raise, and yes, I gave her the promotion. Our deal is over; I don't owe you anything anymore."

* * *

How horrible! How do you think she felt? How would you feel if this happened to you? Completely deflated, I would imagine, as if all the "light" you had just received from your supposed accomplishments had been ripped away from you. And you would probably want to rip your father apart, too.

Why is the person in the story so upset by what her father did? Isn't the most basic of human needs food, water, and shelter? No, it is to be independent, to be a creator.

I previously mentioned that we share the same metaphysical DNA as the Universal Life Force in terms of our desire to be a creator. Does anyone tell God what to? Does God take orders from anyone? NO! God is cause, not the effect. Therefore, we, too, hate to be told what to do. We love being in control. Given all of this, one of the greatest desires of a human being is the overwhelming need to be the cause, to be able to say, "I made it happen."

Bridge #3: I made it happen; I am cause. (BREAD OF SHAME)

Infinite and enduring fulfillment can only be yours if you work for it. Nothing that you get for free belongs to you. The UNIVERSAL WISDOM calls this BREAD OF SHAME.

What it basically means is that anything you get or have that you did not earn comes with strings attached. Payment for taking something you didn't earn or create usually takes the form of pain, suffering, and chaos.

There are times, however, when we do receive things we don't "work" for. The UNIVERSAL WISDOM explains that payback from the "light" we created in previous lifetimes can manifest in current ones. The goal is not to ride on the coattails of some hoped-for windfall from a previous lifetime. It is to live in the present and be the creator and cause of every moment in the here and now.

Think of the Universal Truth of BREAD OF SHAME as a bank account that spans lifetimes. Each time you earn and create "light", it's deposited into your BREAD OF SHAME bank account, to be withdrawn whenever you are in times of need. Most likely, you don't know what type of reserve you created in past lifetimes, so start now. Earn and work for your "light" so you can begin to deposit into your BREAD OF SHAME account.

Let me give you some examples to clarify this very important **bridge** (I made it happen; I am cause) to the *Infinite Realm*. I'm pretty sure you don't remember learning to feed yourself as a baby. You started off being fed a bottle. Then you smacked the bottle away because you wanted to hold it yourself. Then you started drinking from a cup. Then it went from your being fed solids, to your—one more time—smacking away the hand that fed you, and eventually, to your feeding yourself.

Your parents dreaded this rite of passage, as they knew there was going to be a big mess. But you wouldn't eat unless you held the spoon. The food went everywhere but in your mouth. It went into your ear, hair, eyes, all over your face until you mastered feeding yourself. But there was one thing you were absolutely sure about: you wanted to feed yourself.

So, what was stronger, the desire to be the creator/cause, or the hunger? When the baby finally gets that spoon in his grubby little hands, there will be a big mess, but the baby will be so happy! This is the destiny of all human beings, to be happy when they are in charge, when they are the cause and creator of their life.

How do babies learn how to walk? They fall down and then get up, fall down and get up, one million, trillion, gazillion times. Do the babies ever complain? Never. They don't even cry. I remember biting my nails and holding my breath every time my babies fell, and prayed that they didn't hurt themselves. OMG, it hurt to watch them, but they had a single-minded determination. When they finally stood up and took that first step, they had the biggest grins on their faces! Why? Because they could say, or babble, "I did it myself. I made it happen."

Have you ever had friendships or situations in which you had really gone out of your way to help someone and that person eventually turned on you? You tortured yourself, asking yourself over and over again, "What did I do? I don't understand. I was nothing but kind to that friend. What happened? I did everything for this person. I helped. I took. I cooked. I picked up their kids from school. I listened to them. Why aren't they my friend anymore?"

Simple: BREAD OF SHAME. You gave too much, helped too much. Fundamentally, you emasculated them. You didn't allow them the opportunity to work things out on their own. To be the creator of the solution to their challenge. Even though it is a natural human tendency to take the easy way out, eventually, on a subconscious level, the taker knows that an imbalance is being created (BREAD OF SHAME), and it has to stop.

If you, the giver, continue to give too much, the taker won't be able to say, for example, they got through the divorce on their own, they created the support systems they needed, they got the professional counseling they needed, and they grew and learned the lessons they needed to learn from the marriage. If they can get through the divorce process as a creator, then they can earn the right to a new beginning.

I remember, I had a very good friend who was going through a divorce. Because I had already gone through one, she relied heavily on me for support. I gave too much; I was always there for her. I created BREAD OF SHAME and a few months in, she stopped calling, and now we are no longer friends. I was so hurt. I couldn't understand why she dropped me. My point is that even though I felt like I was doing something kind and good, and, yes, it is my nature to be a giver—in this case, giving too much was not the way for me create "light."

I learned a huge lesson. I can never be responsible for taking away an opportunity from someone to create their own solution to a given challenge. I can be a source of support, but not *do it* for someone else. It hurts both me and the taker. The UNIVERSAL WISDOM shares that creating BREAD OF SHAME for yourself and others hits you in the pocketbook. And finally, when you do it for someone else, you prevent that person from building a much-needed **bridge** to the *Infinite Realm*.

There is an art to achieving a balance between giving and receiving. We'll talk about that in Chapter 14.

So, if giving too much is not good, then it stands to reason that taking too much is no good either. How many times have you heard about rock stars, sports figures, and actors imploding/exploding via suicide, drug overdoses, excessive spending, multiple sexual partners, DUIs, etc.? They have generous resources, and can buy whatever they want and create whatever they want, and yet they are still checking out.

Look, I'm not judging or condemning anyone, and not all celebrities buy into the negative aspects of materialism. There are many reasons why people give up. No one really knows the reasons why people are driven to take extremely self-destructive actions. I'm just asking, what's missing? What are they looking for?

The UNIVERSAL WISDOM teaches that if you think that selfish materialism will fill you with "light" for the long haul, you will be mightily disappointed. To distract yourself from this crushing disappointment, you might do anything you can to numb the pain, e.g., taking drugs, drinking, having indiscriminate sex, or doing other reckless and dangerous things.

There is no balance in taking too much and giving too much.

And you certainly don't want to be the cause of BREAD OF SHAME in regard to your kids. In my private practice as a concierge life coach, I can't begin to tell you how many times I hear parents complaining about their kids: "I give my kids everything. I don't understand why I have such a challenging time with my children. They don't even want to talk to me. They don't want to know from me. I have done so much for them. I have given them everything;

I've put them through college, bought them cars, put them in private school, and nothing, nada, no communication, no respect, and no appreciation."

So, I'll ask the parents, when your kids were growing up, did you ever make them work for anything, or did you hand them everything? Surprisingly, the parents are flummoxed by this question.

"What do you mean *work?* They're just kids!"

Hello—of course kids can work. Did you ask them to get good grades, pick up their clothes, take out the garbage? That's work. Teaching them how to be a creator starts in infancy. Why? So when they go out into the world, they will be masters at creating, at being cause.

By not encouraging kids to work, no matter their age, you do them a huge disservice.

Why is this? By giving and giving without having them earn, in some fashion, what they want, you set the stage and become responsible for shrinking vessels, for reinforcing their position in the *Finite Realm*.

The ultimate goal in raising children is for them to become independent, responsible creators and to teach them how to build **bridges** to the *Infinite Realm*. They can't do that if their parents give and give without allowing them to earn their way, in one way or another.

Don't you want your kids to know how to take care of themselves? To go out in the world and manage their finances, make meals for themselves, do their own laundry? These questions are important; they are wake-up calls.

I recently attended a parent-teacher conference, and the math teacher, who is really brilliant, told me about the students who are so used to being spoon-fed the material.

"I find myself having to retrain them. Changing their language from, 'Just give it to me and let me get it over with,' to looking at a math problem, analyzing it, and creating a solution."

These kids are not used to logical analysis. Everyone wants it easy. It's human nature not to want to work hard. I am so grateful that my son is in a class with a teacher who is going against the stream, who is forcing him to go deeper, to look within, and to come up with the answer himself. He is learning to be responsible for his learning.

The teacher lets her students "earn" the right answer. Consequently, they own it, they will never forget it, and this builds their self-esteem. The next time they are confronted with a challenge, they get busy taking responsibility to solve the problem. No BREAD OF SHAME.

Wow—so refreshing! Yes, this way of teaching takes more time and effort, and the kids have to sit in the uncomfortable for a lot longer than they would like, but ultimately they win, society wins, and their future mates and children win.

On the flipside, if you succumb to the illusion of taking the easy way out, life quickly loses meaning; boredom, ennui, and disillusionment set in.

Let's go back to story about the woman whose father got her the dream job that she had thought she'd earned on her own merit. My seminar participants ask a lot of questions about the story. They are very confused. They want to know how she should have reacted to the situation, as she didn't *earn* the promotion. Should she even accept the new position? She he has to eat, pay rent, buy gas, afford insurance, etc. She needs the money to support herself. So, what should she do?

She has many choices:

1. She can go talk to her boss, tell him that she's not happy being duped; however, she knows she's worked hard and she still wants what she has earned. She doesn't have to quit. She can still be the creator of her reality. If she's really not needed, she can go find another job. She doesn't have to go all ballistic and crazy. That reaction stems from the *Finite Realm*. If you don't go nuts when things don't go your way, you have a much better chance of building a **bridge** to the *Infinite Realm,* where all possibilities exist.

2. She can quit.

3. She can choose to do nothing and forget the whole thing ever happened. Is that an option? Yes, it is. But she would have to feel good about this choice and not let the bad guy ride her by telling her, "You didn't earn this on your own. Are you sure you really deserve this position?" If she keeps her mouth shut out of fear ("I don't want to lose my job; I need the money"), what will people say? Red flag! This is a *Finite* conversation and eventually it will bite her in the butt.

Or, 4., she can monitor her inner dialogue (**Bridge #1**) and tell herself "It's OK; these are the cards I have been dealt, and I am a loving, caring, sharing creator (**Bridge #2**). I know I can do something amazing with this job, and I am choosing to stay. I am not going to say anything, and I'm going to knock this out of the park." This is coming from an *Infinite* place, not from a *Finite* place, not from a place of resentment. She has to be honest with the way she feels. If she is truly at peace with her choice, then all will be good, but if she feels resentment, mad, sad, depressed, and afraid (**language** of the *Finite Realm*), it will come back to haunt her.

I am going to tell you a story about my son that will shed some light on why it's so important not to be the cause of BREAD OF SHAME for yourself and others.

* * *

Since he was born, I've been teaching my son about the GOOD GUY and the bad guy. I remember when he would throw a tantrum as a little baby, a normal childhood thing. I would turn to him and say, "Who's in control right now, the GOOD GUY or the bad guy?" I was setting the scene, starting the training for him to monitor his inner dialogue (**Bridge #1** to the *Infinite Realm*).

It was much easier to identify the bad guy, as bad guy behavior—throwing tantrums, acting out, etc.—was more visible. At first, I helped him to recognize the bad guy by labeling the negative behavior. I would tell him, "Wow, your bad guy is really in control right now." He learned pretty quickly to identify bad guy behavior. I used to think, *Wow, it's amazing that at two years old, you have mastered the art of monitoring your inner dialogue* (**Bridge #1**)! *You are able to recognize that the bad guy is in control.*

So, when he acted out, I told him, "Great—since the GOOD GUY, the bad guy, and you are one, and I really can't separate the three of you, you are all going to your room for a time-out. When you choose (when you become the cause/creator, **Bridge #3**), to get rid of your bad guy, to kick him out, let me know. When you get rid of your bad guy, you can come downstairs."

I would hear crazy things: doors opening and closing, slamming, banging, and yelling. We had a railing on the second floor that overlooked the first floor. When my son was ready, when he decided that the bad guy had been kicked out, he would pop his head over the railing and ask, "Can I come downstairs now?"

I'd ask him, "Did you get rid of your bad guy?"

He would reply, "I threw him down the stairs," or "I flushed him down the toilet," or "I tossed him out the window," or "I stomped on him."

***

My son learned how to be the cause **(Bridge #3)**, how to monitor his inner dialogue **(Bridge #1)**, and how to take responsibility for his actions. He learned how it felt to be empowered at a very early age. Till this day, when he acts out, I ask him, "Who's in control: the GOOD GUY or the bad guy?" He just needs that verbal reminder to reign himself in.

Also, I did not contribute to creating BREAD OF SHAME for my son. I didn't punish him into submission. I didn't do it for him. There are times when kids need to have consequences, but when you can encourage individuals to regulate their own behavior, this helps to boost their self-esteem and gives them more confidence to continue learning how to master the bad guy.

Whenever you are reactive or feel mad, sad, depressed, afraid, judgmental, etc. (*Finite* **emotions/feelings**), you need to ask yourself, "Who is in control: the GOOD GUY or the bad guy?" This is how you monitor your inner dialogue **(Bridge #1)**, and this is how you begin to gain mastery over the bad guy. It is a very necessary step in connecting to the *Infinite Realm*, the home of Light & Fulfillment.

I know, I know, easier said than done. We are so used to being effect rather than cause: "He did it to me. It's not my fault; I'm a victim." Thinking like this connects us to one place and one place only, the *Finite Realm*, the domain of shrinking vessels.

You want your vessel/soul to expand? Great! Practice using the **Bridges** you already know; monitor your inner dialogue (**Bridge #1**), and when you find yourself thinking, "They made me do it. I don't like it. I don't want it," when you are mad, sad, and depressed (*Finite* **language** and feelings), know that you immediately disconnect from the *Infinite Realm*, the home of Light & Fulfillment.

Instantly catch yourself and say your mantra, "I am a loving, caring, sharing creator" (**Bridge #2**). And remember, by earning and working for everything you get, not only do you get to keep it, you also do not participate in the *Finite* experience of BREAD OF SHAME (receiving something you did not earn).

Bridges to Light & Fulfillment

Bridge:

#1: Monitor your internal dialogue.

#2: I am a loving, caring, sharing creator.

#3: I made it happen; I am cause.

#4:

#5:

#6:

YOU AREN'T HERE TO BE GOOD, YOU ARE HERE TO BE BETTER

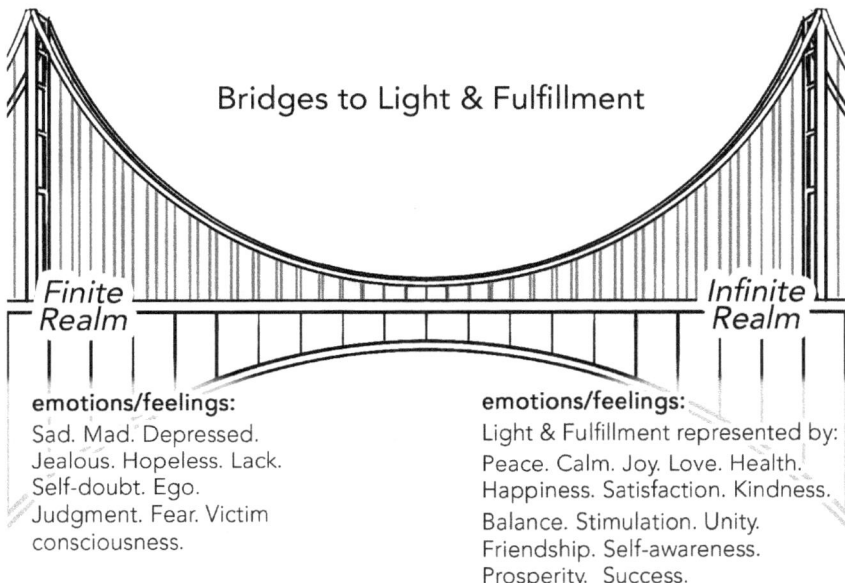

Bridges to Light & Fulfillment

Finite Realm

emotions/feelings:
Sad. Mad. Depressed. Jealous. Hopeless. Lack. Self-doubt. Ego. Judgment. Fear. Victim consciousness.

language:
I want...
I don't like...
I don't want...

body ruled by: bad guy
- five senses
- shrinking vessel
- effect
- BREAD OF SHAME

Infinite Realm

emotions/feelings:
Light & Fulfillment represented by: Peace. Calm. Joy. Love. Health. Happiness. Satisfaction. Kindness. Balance. Stimulation. Unity. Friendship. Self-awareness. Prosperity. Success. Self-expression. Play. Laughter. Soul mates. Creativity. Inspiration. Tranquility. Wisdom. Pleasure. Clarity. Make a difference. To share. Purpose. To serve. Curiosity. Transformation. Excitement. Motivation. Exhilaration. Serenity. Adventure. Spirituality. Compassion. Connection to a Higher Power. Being in the moment. Family. Freedom. Enlightenment.

language:
I am a loving, caring, sharing creator.

soul ruled by: GOOD GUY
- intuition
- expanding soul
- cause
- creator

QUICK REVIEW:

Bridge #3: I made it happen; I am cause. In order to be a creator/cause (which **bridges** you to the "light"), you have to master BREAD OF SHAME. BREAD OF SHAME means you don't receive any fulfillment if something is given to you for free. Furthermore, everything you work for and earn is yours to keep.

In the short term, getting things for free feels great and you buy into the illusion that this "full" feeling will last forever. Do you remember when you bought your first new car? Do you remember laying down the law and telling your family and friends they couldn't eat in the car? Do you remember the new-car smell? Well, I hope you're nothing like me, because after the first week of getting my new car, the kids were eating pizza in it, drinking, and making a huge mess.

Why did I allow this? Because the satisfaction you get from physical acquisitions is short lived. You get a quick "hi" and then "bye-bye." But the satisfaction and fulfillment you get from taking responsibility and creating something from its inception is long lasting and enduring, and no one can take that away from you. You earned it.

Being cause/creator emulates characteristics (loving, caring, sharing, creating) that are in alignment with the *Infinite Realm*. If you do for others without them having earned, you take away their God-given right to create. This is a big no-no.

CHAPTER 7

The Harder the Challenge, the Greater the Fulfillment

When you know the rules of how to create **bridges** to the *Infinite Realm*, life is full of Light & Fulfillment. When you don't know the rules, or you know the rules but refuse to play by them, life is messy, chaotic, and painful. I get it; I don't like anyone telling me what to do either. But in order to thrive and build the necessary **bridges** to get you to the place where all things are possible, you have to play by the rules—no shortcuts allowed.

It is true that your destiny is to receive Light & Fulfillment. It's also true that life is messy, chaotic, and painful. Why? Because we try to circumvent the rules.

You have a choice. You can say, "The world is falling apart, so I might as well be as selfish and materialistic as I want to be right now. I'll do whatever I want that brings me pleasure, and maybe I'll try to do better in the next lifetime. In this lifetime, I'm doing whatever the heck I want. Nothing's going to change; I'm not going to win."

Or, you can learn the rules for acquiring Light & Fulfillment so you can live heaven on earth in this lifetime: First, you have to know, accept, and buy into, that as long as you are having *Finite* conversations and **emotions/feelings** (you are mad, sad, depressed, afraid, etc.), life will always be chaotic, messy, and painful. Second, when you know the rules of how to create **bridges** to the *Infinite Realm*, life is full of Light & Fulfillment.

Work with me as I walk you through the following analogy.

Have you ever wondered why so much shelf space in stores is devoted to all types of games: board games, cards, puzzles, video games, etc.? Simple, we love to play games. I know you have "Monopoly" at home. Which version? Original, Empire, Dinosaur? "All three of them," you say? Why? Can't get too much of a good thing?

What about sports? Do you like hockey? I grew up in a hockey family in Montreal. My father played for the Old-Timers and once played against Guy Lafleur and Ken Dryden in an exhibition game. That was really cool. Every New Year's Eve, we would head to the Montreal Forum for the game of the year, the Russians vs. the Montreal Canadiens, and I will never forget these games. They were often vicious and bloody, players smacked up against the boards, hockey sticks hitting every body part, pucks flying. They were so exciting!

Can you imagine what the game would have looked like if there were no rules? If the players were just told, "Get out on the ice and get the puck in the goal by any means"? If they were only given 10 percent of the rules, like the iceberg analogy where you can only see 10 percent of it protruding from the ocean? What about the rest of rules, the 90 percent?

Playing hockey while knowing only 10 percent of the rules results in utter chaos, violence, and mayhem. The same happens to you when you live life ignorant of the 90 percent, an essential chunk of knowledge that, if you knew it, could prevent a lot of pain and suffering. The bottom line is that when you go through life and you don't know the rules, things get very messy and chaos abounds.

You think you're playing by the rules, but the evidence suggests otherwise. The chaos in your life is a wake-up call, one you need to pay attention to in a timely manner. It's simple: chaos equals "I am in the *Finite Realm*."

Why do you think we like to play games so much? When I ask this question in a seminar, the answer I usually get is, "We play games because we like to win." But upon further discussion, it's agreed that we want the challenge inherent in the game. Think of it this way: If all you wanted was to win, you would play against people who are less skilled than you, and then you would *always* win.

How fun is it to play basketball with someone who can't get the ball in the hoop? How exciting is it to hang out with people who say they are great at cards, but can't even hold them properly in their hands? There is no challenge in that.

Why do you want to win? What is your real motivation? You desire the challenge. Inherent in this desire is the knowledge that there is a chance you might *not* win, you might come up against someone better than you. So, obviously, the winning isn't as important as the challenge. The challenge is more important.

Let's say there is such a huge mess in your garage, it will take a weekend to clean it up. You decide on Friday morning, "That's it; I'm cleaning the garage." When the task is completed, how do you feel? Let's say your kitchen is dirty. You spend an hour cleaning it. When you're done, how do you feel? Let's assume that cleaning the garage brought you a greater sense of fulfillment then cleaning the kitchen did. Why?

UNIVERSAL TRUTH #5
The harder the challenge, the greater the fulfillment.

Please keep in mind that different people have different abilities, and there's no judgment in the examples I am using. Being a stay-at-home mom might be just as hard for someone as becoming a doctor is for another person. The point is that successfully completing any difficult task yields a great feeling of accomplishment. And also, what one considers a difficult chore, another might consider easy.

So, cleaning the garage, you're flying high. With the kitchen cleaned up, you're mildly happy. Again, the greater the challenge, the greater the fulfillment. This is why you push yourself to the limit and challenge yourself to do bigger and greater things. You take chances, you gamble—not at Vegas, but on your life. Subconsciously, on a soul level, you're aware that taking a calculated risk has the potential to translate into a huge revelation of "light."

Why is the chase so exciting? Why is the pursuit of a long-dreamed-of goal so stimulating and motivating? Why do you feel such hope and so alive? Because when you accomplish what you set out to do, you can say, "I did it; I made it happen. I am a creator" (**Bridge #3** to the *Infinite Realm*). And the best part of all? No BREAD OF SHAME.

I want to use my mom as an example. She is a master quilter, and she creates very difficult, intricate patterns. Oftentimes she gets frustrated with their complexity and she has to ditch many efforts and do them over and over again until she gets them right. She joins me for dinner on a weekly basis and shows me all her new creations.

She is so excited. She is so alive. She is so happy. Why? The challenge juices her. It gives her life purpose and meaning. She also is creating an additional **bridge** to the *Infinite Realm*, through **Bridge #2**: I am a loving, caring, sharing creator. How? She lovingly creates her quilts and donates them to cancer patients and victims of Hurricane Irma.

She does what she loves, and then she shares her creations. Wow! What a perfect formula! I love to see someone passionate about what they are doing, someone on fire about their Creation. Are her quilts going to hang in the Smithsonian? Are they going to be heirlooms passed down to the next generations? Probably not, but that's not the point. What matters is that everything you create and share (with a loving, caring, and sharing intention) connects you to the *Infinite Realm*, the home of Light & Fulfillment.

OK, by now, you get the point. You need a challenge in order to move you forward, to stimulate your creative juices, because left to your own devices, you would probably be a couch potato—ha-ha!

CHAPTER 8

Stop the Voices in My Head

The UNIVERSAL WISDOM teaches that we are born into this world (*Finite Realm*) with our very own personal opponent. You've met him before: the bad guy or the false me. I introduced you to him at the beginning of this book. It's time to get better acquainted with him.

His purpose is to maneuver you into behaving in the most selfish and taking ways possible. He tells you to take as much as you want, lie, cheat, steal—and to enjoy it, too. In the heat of the lustful moment, he lulls you into thinking that there won't be any repercussions, moral or otherwise.

He's a sneaky creature. Let's say, for example, you want to buy a pair of shoes, and they are a pair of not-very-practical, red, four-inch stiletto heels. You keep eyeing them as the season goes on, and now they're on sale for 50 percent off, with another 30 percent off of clearance. That's it, done. Under the guise of logic, the <u>bad guy</u> tells you, "Buy them now! You need them. You never know when you can use a four-inch pair of killer heels in red with bling. They're a steal—so worth it!" The argument sounds logical, but the result is that the shoes end up in your closet unused until you can no longer return them or give them away.

There is another voice that wants to be heard, but it's so hard to hear because it is so quiet and noncombative. It's the voice of the GOOD GUY, the real you. The domain of the GOOD GUY is the *Infinite Realm*. The UNIVERSAL WISDOM shares that you're born with these two voices or energetic forces within, and they serve a magnificent purpose in the grand scheme of things. What is their function? Why are they there?

The quiet, almost indistinct voice is the voice of the soul, which knows the way of the "light." It is the white angel that sits on your right shoulder telling you to do good and be good. This is the real you, the GOOD GUY. The other voice is the opponent, the false you that comes from the dark side, and his domain is the *Finite Realm*.

The UNIVERSAL WISDOM teaches us that, unfortunately, the GOOD GUY is dormant, in a state of stasis, if you will, until a girl reaches twelve years of age, and a boy, thirteen years. Because of this, the <u>bad guy</u> has had twelve/thirteen years to practice. He knows every single one of your buttons to push and how to get a rise out of you. The <u>bad guy</u>'s muscles are very big and strong, and he has intimate knowledge of all your strengths and weaknesses.

Then, when you begin puberty, the GOOD GUY wakes up and says in a tiny, weak, quivering voice, "I'm here, I'm ready, and I have some great advice to share with you. I know what your potential is. I know how to **bridge** to the *Infinite Realm*. I'm ready to teach you everything you need to know about living a life of Light & Fulfillment."

The bad guy looks down at the little GOOD GUY and says, "Really? I am going to finish you off! I am stronger than you. Where are your muscles? You know nothing about this person. You have no idea what makes this person tick." The GOOD GUY is at a major disadvantage, and isn't it ironic that all this happens during the erratic teenage years?

Poor, disadvantaged GOOD GUY. It's funny and pathetic all at the same time. Imagine this wimpy weakling standing up to the bad guy in a quiet, shaky voice, trying to assert himself. "I have a suggestion: It probably would be really good if you didn't post that picture on Instagram because you could really hurt someone's feelings." The bad guy rails against every one of the GOOD GUY's suggestions and does everything he can to bully him into submission.

I am so happy I am not a teenager anymore because over the next couple of years, these teenagers have to really learn how to corral the bad guy. Yeesh, not easy! And here we are, most of us out of our teenage years, and we are still trying to bludgeon the bad guy into submission.

Remember the story I shared with you about how I taught my son about the GOOD GUY and the bad guy? Whenever he acted out, I would ask him, "Who is in control: the GOOD GUY or the bad guy?" (monitoring your inner dialogue, **Bridge #1** to the *Infinite Realm*). You, too, need to ask yourself this question every time you feel mad, sad, depressed, afraid, and hopeless (**emotions/feelings** of the *Finite Realm*). This is the first step in constructing the **Bridge.** You take personal responsibility and create an internal locus of control.

You're never going to get rid of the bad guy, but you can learn to corral him. This is part of your transformational work, an essential part of becoming the best version of yourself. I know; battling the bad guy for the rest of your life; not fun. Just like the expression "no pain, no gain," I promise you, it gets easier, and each time you subdue your bad guy, you will feel like you've conquered the world.

One day I got a call from my son's teacher. She said, "I really need to talk to you. I am very concerned about your son; he kind of talks to himself." When I asked her to give me an example, she told me the following story.

"One day he was taking a test, and I heard him mumbling to himself. I went over to him and I explained that he needed to be quiet because other kids were also taking the test and they needed to stay focused.

"When I asked him, 'Why are you talking to yourself?' he replied, 'I'm telling the bad guy to leave me alone. He is bothering me, telling me I don't know what I'm doing, and that I'm not going to pass the test, so I'm telling him to shut up.'"

After telling me the story of this exchange she had with my son, the teacher asked me, "Mrs. Deakter, is there something I should know? Does your son have any psychological issues I should be made aware of?"

No, he's not crazy, just like you are not crazy when you hear the GOOD GUY and bad guy go at it.

I said to my son's teacher, "He's telling the bad guy to leave him alone. I think it's a pretty good thing, don't you? It shows a lot of maturity and an ability to understand his inner dialogue" **(Bridge #1)**.

She was suitably impressed; however, I did tell my son to keep it under wraps in the future. So, yes, if you go around verbalizing your inner dialogue between the GOOD GUY and the bad guy, you will probably get into trouble. Censorship in this situation is a good thing.

The bad guy is not you. I say that because the UNIVERSAL WISDOM teaches us that the Higher Power/God/Universal Light Force is good, and since we all have a Godlike spark within, we too are good. We are all children of that force. The bad guy is not your true essence. Your true essence is good.

So why do you need to have a bad guy to become a better person? you may be thinking. It would be so much easier if things went smoothly and there were no challenges. Really? Maybe for a little while, but soon, you would get really bored. I remember friends telling me that when they were in between jobs, they got less done than while they were working. They couldn't understand that dynamic. Human nature is to produce more when we are under some pressure or deadline. For most of us, without an opponent/challenge/pressure, we don't move.

So the real game, the real challenge, is the battle that happens within, pitting the real you against the false you.

It is the voice in your head, the bad guy, telling you that you are no good, you don't stand a chance, and you'll never make it. But you will make it; you will win. Eventually, it will get easier to move yourself to action before the bad guy gets involved. This will alleviate a lot of chaos and create a "new normal" relationship with the bad guy, where, when he does show up, his interference will be less invasive and more manageable.

CHAPTER 9

I'm Not Buying What You Have for Sale

It's time to get down to business and let the <u>bad guy</u> know who's boss. You need to know when the <u>bad guy</u> is coming out to play, identify him immediately, and put the kibosh on him. In this chapter, I will introduce you to a game-changing technique that will empower you to do just that. It is called the **4-Step Creator Process**.

The first step is to recognize when the <u>bad guy</u> is coming out to play. Clients often ask me: "How do you know which 'guy' is talking?" That's a truly important question. You need to know how to differentiate between the two voices.

Let's keep it simple and brilliant. Ask yourself the following questions: "Where am I coming from? Am I coming from judging, hating, self-doubt, lack, or fear (*Finite Realm*)?" If yes, then evil, chaos, and a disconnect from the "light" is the result. Your affinity is with the opponent, the bad guy in the *Finite Realm*.

Or are you coming from a desire to love, care, share, and create (*Infinite Realm*, GOOD GUY)? Are you buying extra quilting material because you're afraid it won't be there if you should need it sometime in the future (*Finite Realm*, bad guy)? Are you acting out of lack and scarcity (*Finite Realm*, bad guy), or are you buying the fabric with the intention of donating a quilt to a needy cause in the foreseeable future (*Infinite Realm*, GOOD GUY)? Are you going away on vacation because you can't take it anymore (*Finite Realm*, bad guy)? Or are you are taking the vacation because you need to go and rejuvenate so you can come back and share more and care more (*Infinite Realm*, GOOD GUY)?

Whenever your actions, feelings, and thoughts lead you in a direction that is loving, caring, sharing, and creating, walk that path. But if your actions, feelings, and thoughts have the potential to create madness, sadness, depression, fear, and chaos, do not walk that path.

> This evil inclination (bad guy) is just a guest, a passerby, it's not the real you. If he sees that the door is open, he'll walk in. He'll stand in the entrance; if nobody tells him to leave, he'll goes to the living room. If nobody tells him to leave, he'll take food from the kitchen. If nobody says anything, he'll climb into your bed, throw you out, and take over. (Midrash Rabbah, Bereshith 22:6)

I have a student who moved to Florida from New Jersey and worried about the transition for her fourteen-year-old son. As a single mother, she faced the tough decision of whether to enroll him at boarding school in New Jersey, where he could be with his childhood friends, or to keep her small family intact by insisting that he make the move with her. Her dilemma: What was best for her boy?

I was so touched and impressed by her strength and ability to recognize his needs and put them first, especially since her natural desire would be to have her child by her side. This was a pure and true act of loving, caring, and sharing.

Can you imagine the conversation going on in her head? The bad guy saying, "Don't do it! You're crazy! Your kid is going to be alone. Who's going to watch out for him? You're the best person to advocate for him! Why are you putting him in somebody else's hands?" Wow, and ouch! The bad guy hit every button, every fear of a mother. The GOOD GUY, on the other hand, says, "I know New Jersey is going to be the best place for him. It's a hard age. He's a teenager; he needs consistency. He'll have his friends. He'll be safe. He'll get the best education."

There is no right or wrong formula. If you want to **bridge** to the *Infinite Realm*, the bottom line is that you must check in with your inner dialogue (**Bridge #1**). It's about confronting your bad guy, your inner demons. I know and agree that it is so hard to look inside. You'd sometimes rather get a root canal, ha! This is the real war, the real battle. It's internal, not external. It exists within each one of us, pitting the real you/GOOD GUY against the false you/bad guy.

What I am going to introduce to you now (**Bridge # 4**) will help you to clearly differentiate between the voices of the real you/GOOD GUY and the false you/bad guy. More importantly, you will learn how to master and corral the bad guy.

The 4-Step Creator Process

A situation/challenge arises that makes you very upset. It's instinctual human behavior to get reactive and feel mad, sad, depressed, judgmental, and afraid (*Finite Realm*). But you already know that this breaks your **bridge** to the *Infinite Realm*. It cuts you off from Light & Fulfillment—not a good thing. How do you build a **bridge** back to the *Infinite Realm* during times of intense challenge? Back and forth, back and forth over the **bridge** from the *Finite Realm* to the *Infinite Realm*. We should be really skinny by now, with all this activity—ha-ha!

STEP #1:

Monitor your inner dialogue (**Bridge #1**) and recognize that you are being reactive to a *Finite* thought or feeling. You're afraid, mad, sad, depressed, judgmental of yourself or someone else.

I love using this example: You're in the supermarket. You have eleven items in your cart and you're in a ten-item lane. The woman behind you is eyeing your cart. She's edgy and nudgy and keeps looking over your shoulder. Her energy is de*finite*ly telling you that she's upset. Eventually, she just can't help herself and says, "Lady, you've got more than ten items in your cart." You're already defensive and on edge; you're not at your calmest and it won't take much to tip you over the edge.

What's coming up for you? How do you feel? What are you thinking? If nothing else, recognize that you are feeling reactive, and not in a good way. You might be thinking, "Who are you to tell me what to do? Don't you have something better to do with your life than count the items in my cart?" The moment you recognize that you are having a *Finite* moment, you've won.

You also need to recognize when you are judging yourself and directing negativity inward. An example of this would be someone who has a poor body image and thinks they are fat. When a person wakes up in the morning and looks in the mirror and all they see is a chunky person, this can send them on a downward spiral emotionally for the whole day. They can think some really terrible things: "I'm ugly. I'll never find my soul mate. I'm never going to lose weight; it's impossible!" Their self-confidence takes a nosedive and this affects all aspects of their life. Once the bad guy has you hooked in this loop, it is so hard to recognize the pattern. Negative emotions are really hard obstacles to overcome. You can't let the bad guy win. Awareness is the first step of the **4-Step Creator Process**.

STEP #2:

Acknowledge that the reactive thought or feeling is coming from the dark side. It's the work of the false you/bad guy. If you think it's the real you, the bad guy has won. How? By keeping you in victim consciousness: "I made a mistake and I'm never going to be able to fix it. I can't pull myself up. I've failed again. I'm never going to lose weight. I keep failing over and over again." This is the **language** of the *Finite Realm*.

Actually, making friends with failure is not such a bad idea. The UNIVERSAL WISDOM clearly teaches that a wise man falls seven times and picks himself up again. Without failure/challenges, you would not be able to grow and transform into the best version of you. Failure is actually written into humanity's spiritual DNA, so we could choose to reinvent ourselves, to "just do it," until we get it right. You will feel so good when you are able to say, "I did it. I turned darkness into light."

In the beginning, if all you can do is recognize/acknowledge that you are having a negative, reactive thought, it's all good. Eventually you will be able to pinpoint which negative thought you are having: mad, sad, depressed, judgmental, hurt, jealous, or afraid, etc.

STEP #3:

STOP! Put the brakes on the negative thought, feeling, or action. Imagine a stop sign, or pulling back on the reigns of a horse, or whatever imagery works for you. Stop, not suppress, because suppressing makes us sick. Take a breather; put distance between yourself and that *Finite*, negative thought. When the negative thought or action knocks on your door, you don't have to answer. You don't have to buy what the bad guy has for sale. It's totally up to you.

I am a champion equestrian, and I remember that, at times, I was so afraid. "How am I, a little nothing (weight-wise, in comparison to my horse), going to control him?" I had to keep reminding myself that I had years of experience to understand that I was a great rider. No matter what happened, all I had to do was pull on the reins and the horse would stop. All you have to do is use the tools you are learning, and you, too, can "pull on the reins" and get the bad guy to stop.

STEP #4:

Bring in the "light." Ask yourself the question, "How am I going to react to the challenge so that I am responsible for building a **bridge** to the *Infinite Realm*, where I can download Light & Fulfillment?"

In the case of the nosy shopper behind you, will taking the onion out of your cart and throwing it at her connect you to the *Infinite Realm*, the home of Light & Fulfillment? Of course not! How about giving her the benefit of the doubt (*Infinite Realm*)? Maybe she's in a hurry, or maybe she's on the way to the hospital. Or you could say, "I'm so sorry; I have too many items in my cart. Would you like to go ahead of me?" Or you can ignore her. Is ignoring her going to create "light"? No! It might escalate things.

There are multiple ways you can deal with the challenge, but is it really worth fighting over an onion—raising your blood pressure and risking your physical and mental health?

OK, I know I am using a somewhat simplistic example. I know that there are much bigger fish to fry, and humanity faces much greater challenges than a nosy person looking over your shoulder into your shopping cart.

You've got to start somewhere. Think of it this way: When you master the <u>bad guy</u> with the small stuff, you build your GOOD GUY muscles to deal with the bigger stuff. It's trial and error, so be kind to yourself; you've only just begun to build your GOOD GUY muscles. Take heart in knowing that doing it over and over until you get it right is written into your spiritual DNA.

Becoming reactive is a normal response. It's a human response. This is a general rule of thumb, and it usually goes in increments of three. If you're very reactive, even after taking a step back, wait three seconds, wait three minutes, wait three hours. It could take three months, three years, or three lifetimes. Sometimes it takes that long to bring in the "light." Sometimes you have relationships with people that are so toxic, so negative, that bringing in the "light" can take a lot of time. But just know it's not about the length of time; it's about constantly recommitting: "I am fighting. I choose to overcome my <u>bad guy</u>." And each time you do that, no matter how long it takes, the Universal Light Force will deliver into your hands every tool you need to win the war.

We get supernal verification for this. There is a famous sentence in the Old Testament that says, "When you will go out to war against your enemies, the Lord your God will deliver them into your hand …" (Bible, Deuteronomy, 21:10) What does this mean? Successfully overcoming a challenge doesn't mean that you necessarily have to physically "go to war." You don't have to have a fistfight. You don't have to confront, and you don't have to go to court.

You first decide in your mind; you make the decision, "I am going to attack this challenge head on. I have no idea how; my enemies can be huge. I am this one little guy and there's a huge army over there with guns and cannons."

Who are you really fighting? Is it the platoon with the newest and greatest tanks? No, you fight fear, anxiety, doubt, and negativity, the <u>bad guy</u> within, the false you, the voice in your head that tells you, "You're never going to overcome this illness. You're never going to overcome this financial challenge. You're never going to heal this broken relationship. You're never going to find your soul mate." That's the war.

The minute you choose to fight, the person you need to go to court with calls and says, "Let's settle." The person you need to have a conference with about your kid calls up and says, "No worries, we found a solution." You meet a friend in the supermarket and she tells you of a doctor she just saw, and that's just the type of doctor you have been looking for.

My students and clients at this point say, "But how do you find the strength? I'm so tired from fighting all the time!" You need to change your relationship with the word "fight." Fighting doesn't have to have negative connotations.

See yourself as a leader, creator, or one who manifests. When you are going through a rough patch, you can choose to lead your way through the darkness toward the "light" at the end of the tunnel. You can create a solution that has a positive outcome. Stay focused on building those **bridges**. Know that when you win the war, the reward is Light & Fulfillment. That should be a great motivator and a source of comfort.

Mastering the bad guy is being able to see the movie of all the possible outcomes and choosing the one that will create "light." This isn't easy to do in the heat of the moment. I highly suggest you use **Bridge #3** and say to yourself, "I am a loving, caring, sharing creator." Say it as many times as you need. It will reveal to you the right way to bring in the "light."

This mantra should be like a quiet recording in the background of your mind. Say it over and over, as it will keep open the corridor to the *Infinite Realm*—the home of Light & Fulfillment and the solution to all of life's challenges.

I, too, use the **4-Step Creator Process**. First, I recognize the recording, the bad guy's voice telling me all the negative bullcrap that I've heard a million times before. I use my "I am," statements (**language** of the *Infinite Realm*), and I have tons of them. For example, I can get up in front of thousands of people and speak, but I don't like to go to social gatherings by myself. As a doctor, my husband works long hours, and many times I have to attend social and business events alone. I hate it, and my bad guy works me: "Who are you going to talk to? You won't know anyone. You're going to be holding up the wall."

So I do a full stop, and I bring in the "light" with my "I am" statement created for this specific scenario. It goes like this, "I am effervescent, bubbly, and scintillating company. I am surrounded by like-minded people, and I am having a great time." The bad guy can take us down in three seconds flat, before we even start the day, but the moment you say, "I'm going to fight," you've won.

And if you wake up in the morning feeling fat, you can use the following "I am" statement: "I am beautiful just the way I am, as the Higher Power made me this way. I release weight with ease. I am a lean, clean 'light' machine."

During times of unrest, use "I am" statements as a vehicle to transform into the best version of yourself. Words have power. How was the world created? According to the Old Testament, God said, "Let there be light . . . " (Bible, Genesis 1:3)

Words have power. There is an expression: be very careful what you ask for, because you just might get it. Most of you are familiar with the word "abracadabra." It is commonly used as an incantation by magicians when they are performing a magic trick. What is its origin? Why is it so widely used and recognized? I turn to Hebrew, as the language of Creation, for the answer. "Abracadabra" is derived from Hebrew and means, "I will create as I speak." How cool is that?

Use the power of the word to **bridge** to the *Infinite Realm*. Keep all communication in the positive, and start all statements with "I am" (the **language** of the *Infinite Realm* and one of God's holy Hebrew names, *Ehyeh*).

Following are some examples of how to use the **language** of Creation to connect to the *Infinite Realm*. Use them as a template to create your own tailor-made "I am" statements for each challenge.

1. I am good. I am a holy child of the Universal Light Force. I am good because the Higher Power is good. (All challenges come from God; therefore, they are good, too, and they are for my highest good and potential.) I am open to receive healing, blessings, guidance, and abundance in all areas of my life.

2. If it be Thy holy will.

3. Thank you, my Holy Creator, for all the blessings you have given me and the blessings you will continue to give me.

4. I am your holy daughter/son _____.
   (Insert your name.)

Its components are the following:
1. I am open to receive.
2. Acknowledge that it is the Higher Power's job to determine what is in your highest good.
3. Express gratitude.
4. End by acknowledging your unique relationship to the Universal Light Force.

I cannot do such a broad subject justice here. Explaining how to create these life-altering "I am" statements can fill a whole book. Please contact me personally if you would like assistance working on this practice.

Bridges to Light & Fulfillment

Bridge:
#1: Monitor your internal dialogue.
#2: I am a loving, caring, sharing creator.
#3: I made it happen; I am cause.
#4: 4-Step Creator Process.
#5:
#6:

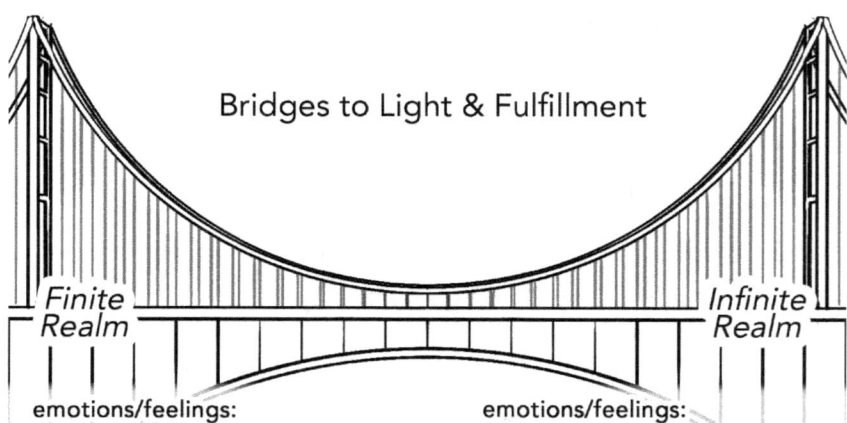

Bridges to Light & Fulfillment

Finite Realm

emotions/feelings:
Sad. Mad. Depressed. Jealous. Hopeless. Lack. Self-doubt. Ego. Judgment. Fear. Victim consciousness.

language:
I want...
I don't like...
I don't want...

body ruled by: <u>bad guy</u>
- five senses
- shrinking vessel
- effect
- BREAD OF SHAME
- reactive

Infinite Realm

emotions/feelings:
Light & Fulfillment represented by: Peace. Calm. Joy. Love. Health. Happiness. Satisfaction. Kindness. Balance. Stimulation. Unity. Friendship. Self-awareness. Prosperity. Success. Self-expression. Play. Laughter. Soul mates. Creativity. Inspiration. Tranquility. Wisdom. Pleasure. Clarity. Make a difference. To share. Purpose. To serve. Curiosity. Transformation. Excitement. Motivation. Exhilaration. Serenity. Adventure. Spirituality. Compassion. Connection to a Higher Power. Being in the moment. Family. Freedom. Enlightenment.

language:
I am a loving, caring, sharing creator.

soul ruled by: <u>GOOD GUY</u>
- intuition
- expanding soul
- cause
- creator
- proactive

QUICK REVIEW:

Bridges to Light & Fulfillment

> **Bridge #1:** Monitor your internal dialogue.
> **Bridge #2:** I am a loving, caring, sharing creator.
> **Bridge #3:** I made it happen; I am cause. (no BREAD OF SHAME)
> **Bridge #4:** 4-Step Creator Process.

Life is a game, and what do you need when you have a game? You need a challenge. You also need an opponent, and who is the opponent? The opponent is the false you/<u>bad guy</u> that talks to you negatively: "You can't do this. Who do you think you are. You are never going to make it. You are not good enough." It's part of your personality, but it's not part of your soul. If things are too easy, there's no challenge—which ultimately leads to complacency and stagnation. And guess who wins?

Without an opponent/challenge—no pain, no gain—will you move? Will you feel the urgency to transform? Unfortunately, for the most part, transformation happens only when we are pushed and in pain. It's the rare person who says, "Bring it on." That's just the way it is. The path of mediocrity is very attractive. The easy way out isn't the path to happiness, to Light & Fulfillment.

4-Step Creator Process

This is a step-by-step guide on how to master the bad guy and overcome challenges. Why do you need it? To create a **bridge** to the *Infinite Realm*, the home of Light & Fulfillment.

STEP #1:

Recognize that you are having a negative thought and reaction: "I don't like this person. I don't like what this person did to me. I am a loser, etc." This is the **language** of the *Finite Realm*. Remember the example of being in the supermarket with eleven items in the ten-item lane? How are you going to react when the lady behind you starts sticking her nose in your business?

STEP #2:

Acknowledge that the negative thoughts and feelings are coming from the false you/the bad guy. This is not the real you.

STEP #3:

Stop! Seize the negative thought, feeling, or emotion, and take a breather to prevent your bad guy from becoming engaged. Once the false you is engaged, it's game over; the *Finite Realm* rules supreme. This is not something you want. It disconnects you from the *Infinite Realm*, the home of Light & Fulfillment.

STEP #4:

Bring in the "light." Use **Bridge #3**: I am a loving, caring, sharing creator. Seriously, this **language bridges** you to the *Infinite Realm*, the reservoir of all solutions to life's challenges. Say it over and over again until you no longer feel like ripping off someone's head or doing damage to yourself in the form of some extremely negative self-talk.

It takes time to learn how to master this Process. Be kind to yourself. Everyone is different and will master each step at his or her own pace. Life is not a race. If you are moving forward, then you are not moving backward; all is good.

CHAPTER 10

Everything Happens for a Reason

Do you believe that the challenges that arise in your life are random occurrences? Are you just like a leaf blowing in the wind, going wherever the wind takes you? The UNIVERSAL WISDOM teaches that there is no such thing as coincidence; everything happens for a reason. Unfortunately, when you are ruled by the <u>bad guy</u> and rooted firmly in the *Finite Realm*, you don't see the seed, the reason why the challenge is happening.

Eventually you will know why you had to go through the challenge, but you might not know why in this lifetime. You might see the cause in the next lifetime or the lifetime after that.

The UNIVERSAL WISDOM teaches that we come into this world with a predetermined destiny.

Destiny is the movie that you are born with. It is the movie that includes all the challenges/opportunities you need to overcome your negative character traits that prevent you from becoming a better you. It is the process whereby you will reach your full potential.

I am not telling you that you have no choice in this process. Your life's purpose and mission are predetermined, but you get to choose how you accomplish them: as a creator or a victim. There is free will in how you react to all the challenges along the way. You choose the movie that gets you from point A to point B. The goal is to choose the movie that gets you through the challenge in the shortest amount of time with the least amount of pain, suffering, and chaos. That choice is yours to make.

When the wave (challenge) comes, use all your tools and choose whichever **bridge** will work in the moment. It could be that you need to use a combination of **bridges**, or just one of them, but don't give up. If you give up and choose to let the bad guy win, the intensity and duration of the challenge gets dragged out, and it can even be extended into the next lifetime.

Do you choose to build the **bridge** from the *Finite Realm* to the *Infinite Realm,* or do you choose to be reactive and cry, "Woe is me"? How do you deal with the hand you are dealt? Are you mad, sad, depressed, and afraid? "Why me?!" No one is trivializing the challenges you have to deal with. They are tough and scary, and they can seem insurmountable. These challenges are of paramount importance. They are what you have to go through, as they will shape and mold you into the fulfilled person you are destined to be.

"Losing it," is part of being human. Why? So we can pick ourselves up, learn from our mistakes, and move on. When darkness falls and it looks hopeless, there is always a way out.

Yes, it's easier to tremble and complain, but truly, your best proactive choice is to focus on building **bridges** to the *Infinite Realm*. You will learn and grow, and all of humanity will benefit. Do you think that the Light & Fulfillment you created stays only with you?

No, you inspire everyone. They look at you and see you overcoming, see you thriving in the face of adversity, and they go, "Wow! If she can do it maybe I can, too." "Look at him; he's a regular, normal person. I am a regular, normal person. If he can do it, I can do it." People love to hear stories of how others overcame challenges. It feels right and authentic. It connects us to our true self. People want truth because truth is inspiring.

When you hear people telling stories of their triumphs, you can actually see the Light & Fulfillment and wonder on their faces. And you know what the best part of all of this is? Each time you successfully build a **bridge**, it builds your confidence and belief in your ability to keep building **bridges** from the *Finite Realm* to the *Infinite Realm* each time a challenge occurs. It reacquaints you with that intoxicating, heady, euphoric feeling that there is hope for a better tomorrow.

FYI, this is what a miracle is. It's the ability to jump/**bridge** from the *Finite Realm* to the *Infinite Realm*. It's traveling through the wormhole into the reality where Light & Fulfillment is possible. All miracles are created in the *Infinite Realm*.

To ground all of this and make it more concrete and tangible, my students and clients oftentimes ask me to give real-life examples of how this all works. I have many stories to share. Have I seen people heal from major illnesses? Yes. Have I seen people rise from financial ruin? Yes. Have I seen impossible relationships get better? Yes. However, the stories I'm choosing to share are deliberately light in nature because the long and involved "miracle" stories require more time to tell than this forum provides.

CLIENT #1:

This is how you know the Universe is looking out for you. Such a weird story! Yesterday I had such a craving for jelly beans, so I bought a box of Mike and Ike candies—yum! The next morning, I was asked to drive a friend to the airport. I did it. Hey, I'm always on the lookout for adding brownie points to my spiritual bank account; it only benefits me and is the greatest security net. As I dropped my friend off, I noticed there was a bag of jelly beans in the car, and I asked him if he wanted to take them on the plane. He told me no, I could eat them if I wanted to. I'm thinking to myself, *Yum*, but they are fattening and I am on a diet (again). As I bite into one, the crown on my tooth falls off. What the heck—so weird. As always, there are no accidents; everything happens for a reason. My dentist saw me immediately and was able to put the crown back on, and while I was there, they found a cavity in the early stage, so I got it painlessly filled. I think my jelly beans were gentle, merciful angels to get me to the dentist before the cavity got worse.

CLIENT #2:

Serendipity, ahhhh!!! What a beautiful reminder that you are in balance, that chaos is not running the show. My husband told me the blow-dryer was broken, and I immediately went into meltdown mode, thinking, *Ugh, another thing to put on my to-do list!* With a resigned shrug, I headed off to the hairdresser, and as I was sitting in the chair, a sales rep approached my hairdresser and asked him if he needed anything: a curling iron, a blow-dryer? My ears perked up. I looked at my hairdresser questioningly, and I said, "I need a blow-dryer. Can I buy one?" Ahhhh!!!! Without even having to do the work, the perfect professional blow-dryer fell right into my lap. How did this happen? Thank you, Shoshana, because as soon as I started to freak out, I used the mantra "I am a loving, caring, sharing creator," and the blow-dryer effortlessly appeared. I could use more of that.

CLIENT #3:

We've recently discovered that my son has allergies. The doctor wanted him to try a specific product, which meant I had to make a special trip to a specialty health store, and I've been putting it off. You know the drill. So today, I went to my chiropractor's office, and lo and behold, the product I need is prominently displayed in her office for sale. Wow!! No special effort required. There is no such thing as coincidence; everything happens for a reason. Thank you for everything you have taught me. I de*finite*ly feel like I live a fulfilled and protected life where I am in the right place at the right time.

One of my clients asked me a great question: "Being a creator is a characteristic that belongs to the *Infinite Realm,* and it is a behavior that is highly suggested that we adopt, so how can I be a creator if destiny is fixed?" The answer is: You're a creator when you choose to be proactive in how you react to the challenge. You are a creator when you choose to build a **bridge** to the *Infinite Realm* instead of falling on the floor and crying in helplessness and despair. When you choose to build a **bridge**, the challenge is shortened and mitigated.

CHAPTER 11

As Long as You Are Breathing, You Will Be Fixing Something

So, back to destiny. We are not born with a clean slate. Each baby is born unique, with his or her own personality and destiny. We see this with children born to the same family. Each individual is different, even multiple births. Why?

We all come into this life with baggage from previous lifetimes. This "baggage" contains all the negative character traits and scenarios that existed in prior lifetimes, which need to be fixed or corrected. Why? You can't transform into the best version of yourself while holding onto the "baggage" that contains the worst of you. In Hebrew, this fixing is called *tikune*. One of our collective life's purposes is to fix what is broken.

A common reaction to this statement by my students and private clients is, "How do I know what to fix? There are so many things in my life that are 'broken.' What should I be focusing on? How do I know what my *tikune* is? Where do I begin?"

Here are some guidelines for identifying your *tikune/tikunim*. Yes, you can have more than one. Have you ever found yourself in a negative situation that seems to occur over and over again, déjà vu? The only things that change are the names and faces of the people involved and the location in which the event takes place.

Here are some examples:
- You meet someone new, you get close really quickly, and then all of a sudden, the other person loses interest in the relationship.
- Every time you start a business, it fails.
- Every time you walk into a crowd, you become a shrinking violet.
- You support someone during a difficult time in his or her life, and in return, he or she wants nothing to do with you once the trying time is over.
- You get mad every time things don't go the way you think they should.
- You give so much and don't understand why you don't get anything in return.
- People walk all over you because you can't say no.
- You get divorced and remarry someone just like your first partner.

And here's what happens if you choose not to fix what's broken. At that moment, you enter into *Groundhog Day*. If you have not seen the movie, you must see it. It is probably one of the most impactful movies I have ever seen. Bill Murray plays Phil Connors, a TV weatherman. He's selfish, taking, a womanizer, and a schemer. He tries to cheat his way into the job he wants, and he tries get the girl by being an arrogant creep. He wakes up day after day and lives the same day over and over again until he starts to realize, maybe he's got to do something different if he wants a different result.

He's tired of being beaten up. He starts to change, to become more loving, caring, and sharing (**language** of the *Infinite Realm*). Without even knowing it, he begins to build a **bridge** from the *Finite Realm* to the *Infinite Realm*. How do we know when he crosses over? He gets the girl and he earns the job he wants—no BREAD OF SHAME. Once his negative character traits have been fixed, he wakes up to his new life and a better, more improved version of himself.

CHAPTER 12

One, Two, Three Strikes, You're Out

When you are first introduced to your *tikune*, it's usually presented with a mild wake-up call, like a gentle slap on the hand. If you don't listen, the second time you're introduced, you get punched in the face. I liken this process to baseball: one, two, three strikes, you're out. If you refuse to listen, the *tikune* doesn't go away; the Higher Power does. According to the UNIVERSAL WISDOM, God goes into hiding and says, "You know what? You're not ready to do your *tikune*. I'll partner with somebody else who really wants me there to support him or her. When you're ready, I'll be there for you. Never doubt that I'm always there for you, but you need to activate me with your desire to transform into the best version of yourself."

Wake-up calls take on many different forms. Listen and look for them. You know you are more grounded in the *Finite Realm* when the wake-up calls are harsh, like car accidents, life-threatening situations, bad health, and loss of income. Wake-up calls from the *Infinite Realm* are less intense and are infused with mercy.

This is great news. However, since the wake-up calls from the *Infinite Realm* are less severe, you might not listen to them. You may treat them like pesky flies: "Leave me alone; I'm shopping, eating, taking care of my kids, working, cooking, playing." You have to listen, because if you don't pay attention, chances are, you're going to get smashed in the *Finite Realm*.

If somebody calls and tells you, "You know, you hurt my feelings. Please don't do that again," that's a wake-up call. Take it seriously. Don't reply, "You know what? You're too sensitive."

When your child asks, can you read me a story tonight? That's a wake-up call. You might not be spending enough time with your child. "I have three hours of email messages to answer, dishes to wash, clothes to fold, bills to pay, etc." Pay attention. Because you know what happens next? In a couple of years, "Mom, Dad, I was arrested for driving drunk. Come get me out of jail." That's a wake-up call from the *Finite Realm*, one you really don't want. "Mom, Dad, come read me a bedtime story." That's a wake-up call from the *Infinite Realm*, one cloaked in mercy.

I remember when my son used to play soccer as a young child. When he didn't want to play because things weren't going his way, he used to just fall down on the field, cross his arms, and say, "That's it; I'm not playing." You have a choice. You can fall down in the middle of your life, shut down, and say, "I'm not playing." Or you can choose to go through the fear and walk through the pain and be excited about it. Not excited about the challenge, excited that you are going to "fix" something, do your *tikune*. This means you will build a **bridge** to the *Infinite Realm* and gorge on the "light"—yippee! Keep your eyes on the prize.

You cannot escape your destiny. You cannot escape your *tikune*. You are destined to repeat the same mistakes over and over again until you fix them. Yes, you can try to run away. You can run away from a job, a relationship, etc., but you cannot run away from yourself. The same issues will arise time and again until you realize (or not) that you are stuck in a never-ending loop, and that you must do your *tikune*. And what is the benefit of doing your *tikune*? Well, for starters, you won't have to come back/reincarnate, and with each *tikune* that you complete/fix, you get Light & Fulfillment.

Destiny is not something from which you can escape. You can challenge it and turn it into a victory. The Zohar shares that we are so stubborn and fixed in the *Finite Realm,* it could take multiple lifetimes to fix a given *tikune*. Furthermore, if you don't do the *tikune*, the next time it comes around, it will be intensified. Ouch! (Zohar of Vilna, Pinchas P.216b) Why? Obviously the wake-up calls weren't convincing enough, so you will have to come back again and again, with the wake-up calls increasing in intensity until you finally get it right.

UNIVERSAL TRUTH #6
You can't run away from your *tikunim*; you are destined to repeat them until you fix them.

A common question asked by my students is, "But if I complete my *tikune*, does that mean the game is over?" Let's be realistic. Most of us have so many things to fix, we are far from being self-actualized. Typically, when one *tikune* is completed, we quickly start working on another one. As long as you are breathing, you will be fixing something.

In addition, every time you fix something, there is the added benefit of being a creator: you will have no BREAD OF SHAME. You can scream from the rooftops in eternal joy, "I earned this! I made this happen!" (**Bridge #3**) There is no greater feeling than this. You will bask in the glow of a job well done for a while, but sooner rather than later, you will feel the need to start fixing again. The process is similar in structure to a staircase with multiple landings.

You'll work, work, work, work hard and climb the staircase. When your *tikune* is fixed, you will stop on the landing and rest for a while. Soon, you will feel the push to climb again, and then you'll rest and regroup on the landing. Your climb can be vertical or more of a 45-degree slope, and you can go fast or slow.

The only thing that really matters is that as long as you're moving forward, you are not moving backward. Don't get caught up in the speed; life is not a race. And while you are climbing/fixing your *tikune*, you create so much "light" and positive energy that you attract more positivity. You will look and feel transformed. People will see that something is different about you but they won't be able to put their finger on it. They'll ask, "Did you do something different? Did you lose weight? Is that a new hairstyle?"

So you have to do your *tikune* no matter what. Death does not erase your *tikune*. When a person is fulfilled and he finishes his *tikune*, he is the creator of his life. He doesn't need to come back, as he has mastered the game. But if you leave frustrated and empty, you'll be back, and you will get another chance.

The Zohar is widely considered the most important work of Kabbalah, and it says the following about *tikune*:

> Somebody came up to heaven and the angel asked him,
> did you turn the darkness to light and the bitterness into

sweet? If yes, your soul is admitted entrance to heaven; if no, you have to go back and try all over again. What is hell? Hell is when you've passed on, you're outside of your body, you're dead, you look back at the movie of your life, and you see all the times you could've done your *tikune* and you didn't. If you feel the missed opportunities bitterly, don't worry. The bitterness of seeing how close you were and how quickly you gave up, why didn't I fight, how did I mess up all my chances, that is hell. Heaven is when you finish overcoming everything and you master everything. You are free. (Zohar of Vilna, Pinchas P.216b)

Take a moment to identify what your *tikune/tikunim* is/are. Write them down in the space provided.

_____

_____

_____

_____

Bridges to Light & Fulfillment

Bridge:

#1: Monitor your internal dialogue.

#2: I am a loving, caring, sharing creator.

#3: I made it happen; I am cause.

#4: 4-Step Creator Process.

#5: Do your **tikune**.

#6:

YOU AREN'T HERE TO BE GOOD, YOU ARE HERE TO BE BETTER

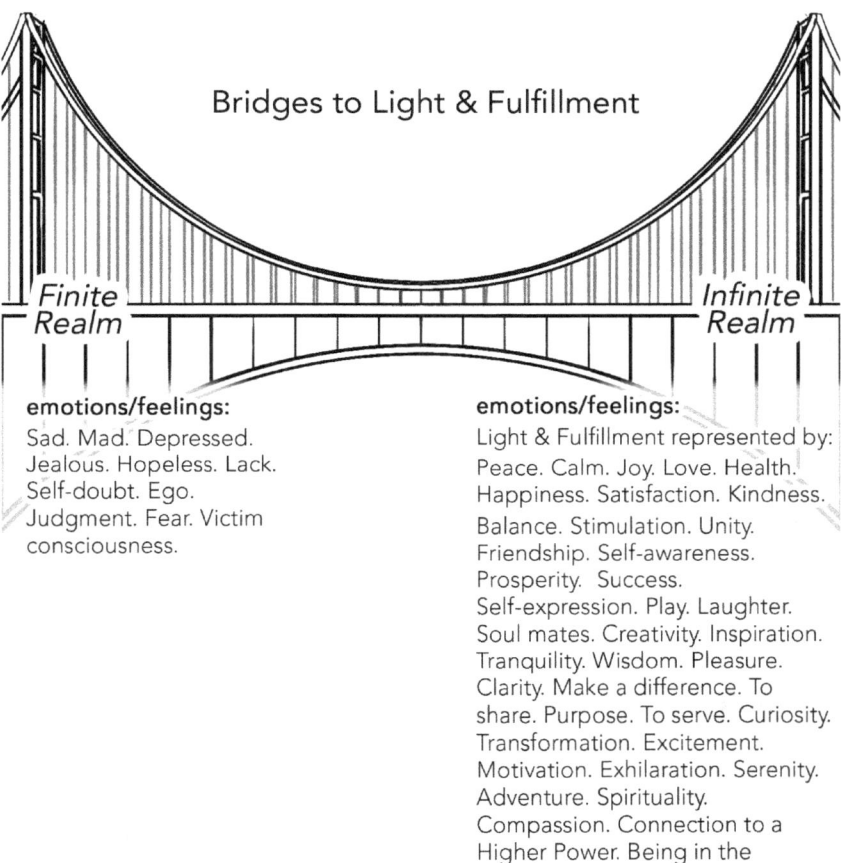

Bridges to Light & Fulfillment

Finite Realm

emotions/feelings:
Sad. Mad. Depressed. Jealous. Hopeless. Lack. Self-doubt. Ego. Judgment. Fear. Victim consciousness.

language:
I want...
I don't like...
I don't want...

body ruled by: bad guy
- five senses
- shrinking vessel
- effect
- BREAD OF SHAME
- reactive

Infinite Realm

emotions/feelings:
Light & Fulfillment represented by: Peace. Calm. Joy. Love. Health. Happiness. Satisfaction. Kindness. Balance. Stimulation. Unity. Friendship. Self-awareness. Prosperity. Success. Self-expression. Play. Laughter. Soul mates. Creativity. Inspiration. Tranquility. Wisdom. Pleasure. Clarity. Make a difference. To share. Purpose. To serve. Curiosity. Transformation. Excitement. Motivation. Exhilaration. Serenity. Adventure. Spirituality. Compassion. Connection to a Higher Power. Being in the moment. Family. Freedom. Enlightenment.

language:
I am a loving, caring, sharing creator.

soul ruled by: GOOD GUY
- intuition
- expanding soul
- cause
- creator
- proactive

QUICK REVIEW:

Tikune: The same negative situation happens over and over again. The only thing that changes are the actors in the play. Our collective destiny is to face challenges head on, using all the tools you've learned so far, to create **bridges** to the *Infinite Realm*, where all the solutions to life's problems exist.

When you have successfully solved your problem, you are able to say, I made it happen. I created another **bridge** from the *Finite Realm* to the *Infinite Realm*, the home of Light & Fulfillment. I am so full of "light" and I feel amazing.

Yes, destiny is predetermined, but you choose how you interact with your challenge. You tell yourself, "You know what, I'm clueless, I don't how to do this; I don't know how to make it through. I have no experience with this, but I choose it." In that commitment, the right answers will come.

What do you do when a challenge arises? Do you react, fall on the floor in the middle of the soccer field and say, "I don't want to play! Game over!"? Or do you use your free will and choose the **4-Step Creator Process (Bridge #4)**?

1. You feel this big, dark wave coming over you, and you have to first recognize that a challenge is coming.

2. Acknowledge how you feel about the challenge. "I'm scared. I can't handle it. I'm mad." It's all good, but don't stay there too long. Remember, mad, sad, depressed, fearful is the **language** of the *Finite Realm*, the home of the bad guy. Get yourself back on track and recognize that all of these feelings come from the false you. It's not really you.

Remember the example of the eleven items in the ten-item lane at the supermarket? Do you really want to be reactive and hit the old lady over the head with your handbag or a baseball bat and/or yell at her to mind her own business? OK, somewhere deep inside, you might still want to, but I'll pretend otherwise, ha-ha! No, the real you is loving, caring, and sharing. The one who wants to bash the old lady on the head is the false you.

3. Stop. Take a step back. Gain some perspective. Reign in the <u>bad guy</u>, and breathe.

4. Bring in the "light." No matter how long this takes, you can't give up fighting. You can't give up until you get to a place of, "I am a loving, caring, sharing creator. Sorry, hyper grocery-item-counting lady in the supermarket, I am giving you the benefit of the doubt. With all due respect, go ahead of me."

Most of the stuff that irritates the crap out of us is really not worth reacting to. Yes, there are really big challenges in life. But to quote a famous expression, don't sweat the small stuff. You're not alone. You have a supernal partner.

Remember, when you choose to fight, the enemy will be delivered into your hands? Winning the battle starts in your mind, the GOOD GUY duking it out with the <u>bad guy</u>. I'm ready to overcome the challenge. I'm ready to become the best version of me.

CHAPTER 13

E.T. Phone Home

According to the UNIVERSAL WISDOM, everything started from an organized and unified place, and everything will arrive back to an organized and unified place (*Infinite Realm*). All the chaos along the way is only temporary, an opportunity for you to perfect.

Without challenges, the <u>bad guy</u>/opponent, would you really feel any compulsion to get off your butt and do your *tikune*? Correct me if I am wrong, but I think you would much rather sit in front of your big-screen TV and veg out, the ultimate in escapism. As of today, the largest TV sold at Best Buy is eighty-eight inches. Before you know it, you are going to live in the TV! You won't ever have to leave your house.

We are all going to go back home to the *Infinite Realm*, some of us faster than others. It all depends on what you desire. If you desire the "light," then you'll do the work, build your spiritual muscles, and create multiple **bridges** to the *Infinite Realm*. You can cross them at will, experiencing multiple episodes of mini heaven on earth.

If you want to give in to the selfish and taking part of your human nature, then it will take you longer to go "home."

For example, you get on the highway at New York and your destination is Miami, an approximate two-day drive. The bad guy distracts you from "**bridge** building," and you exit in North Carolina, and you get stuck there for two or three lifetimes. You finally refocus, pick yourself back up, get back on I-95, and head south. You already know that the bad guy never sleeps, but that doesn't stop you from being diverted once again. This time, you exit in Georgia.

So many starts and stops along the way. It can take many pain-filled lifetimes before you make your way back home to the *Infinite Realm*. Ouch, not my idea of fun!

Everyone is going to get back "home." Your choice is whether you are going to take the "scenic route" or the "super highway."

CHAPTER 14

There Is Order in What Appears to Be All-Consuming Chaos

The world is completely ordered and unified. There is absolute order to what appears to be all-consuming chaos when your vantage point is the *Infinite Realm*. The *Infinite Realm* is well and thriving. It has never gone away; we just don't know how to efficiently access it. This order is a supernal system that was created when God said, "Let there be light," on the first day of Creation.

What "light" is this? It wasn't a physical light, because the moon, sun, and stars were created on the fourth day. This "light" of "Let there be light," this is the "light" we all want. This is the Light of Fulfillment that was broadcasted on the first day of Creation. It has always existed since the beginning of time. It has always been with you, and it is time to reacquaint yourself with it and to reveal it.

There is a sturdy, strong, unwavering metaphysical substructure that supports the world. If you could only see it, its strength and commitment to your finding your way back "home," you would know that you are completely supported and surrounded in the Universal Light Force's loving embrace.

You would know that your destiny is to succeed and thrive, and that you were never meant to falter and drown inde*finite*ly. Know this now, and take from this ancient UNIVERSAL WISDOM the strength, confidence, and courage you need to keep "building **bridges**."

The following example will help to clarify the nature of this supernal support system.

Think about a two-story house. When you stand on the second floor of a two-story house, do you tremble in fear that you're going to fall through the ceiling to the first floor? Do you question whether or not the floor can hold you? No, you trust that the support, the trusses under the floor, are going to hold up the second floor.

There is a system of transcendental trusses that holds up the Universe. We don't trust it because we don't see it. You know that expression, "I'll believe it when I see it"? What do you see most of? Pain, suffering, and chaos. It's time to "see" things differently. And once you do, you will feel embraced, protected, and have faith that this eternal, energetic support structure will never let you down.

You will reconnect with what your soul already knows. The world is structured and deliberately ordered in a perfect way: so that you succeed and are supported in completing your *tikune* and living your life's purpose.

To help make the nature of this hidden support structure concrete, I'm going to give you multiple examples of other systems where the support structure is hidden from the naked eye. The state and health of the support structure of any system can be seen in its physical manifestation. This gives you more information to make better life decisions.

1. Think about a tree. It's big, beautiful, and life-giving. Do you see its root system? No, you have no concept of what's going on beneath the ground. You don't know how wide the root system is and how deep it goes. All you see is the tree, the manifestation/reflection of the roots in the earth. Even though you can't see below the ground to the root system, you can make an educated guess as to the health and stability of the tree. Are the leaves plentiful, lush, and green? Are the branches thick and sturdy? If the answer is yes, then you can accurately presume that the roots of the tree are healthy. The roots are the supporting structure and the tree is its manifestation/reflection.

2. Someone tells you a joke. They want to know if they've made you happy. How would they know? By your laughter and the smile on your face. Your face reflects whether or not you found the joke funny. The question, however, is from where is the emotion of happiness generated? Where is its source? Is it generated from the face? No, it comes from within. So the joy on your face is just a reflection; it's not the source. OK, I get it. Some people are very good at hiding their emotions. But generally, you can gauge the health and well-being/emotional health of a person by the expression on his or her face. Are you dealing with

someone who is happy and open, or mad, sad, and closed? Also of note is the fact that the Hebrew name for face is *panim*, which comes from the same root as the Hebrew word *pnimi,* which means from within. Usually, the expression on the face is a projection of the emotions that are happening on the inside.

3. Where is a computer's brain? It could be on a server, millions of miles away, or it could be under your desk. However, the information you seek is manifested/reflected on the screen of the laptop in your hands.

So how do the above examples apply to you? How do they help you with your life's purpose of "building **bridges**" to the *Infinite Realm* so you can live a life full of Light & Fulfillment?

All of the Universal Truths and **bridges** we have studied in this book have brought you to this moment. This is the culmination of everything we have learned together.

I will now reveal to you how to work within the framework of the supernal, *Infinite Realm* support structure so that you can direct its manifestation/reflection of Light & Fulfillment in the *Finite Realm*. Light & Fulfillment is what all of humanity craves.

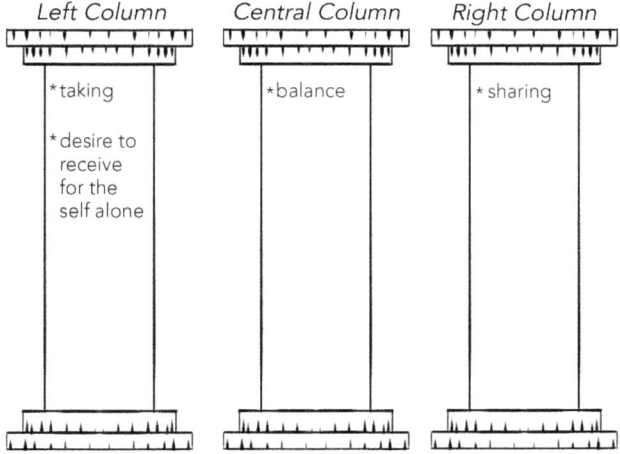

The right column represents the force of sharing. It's characterized by loving, caring, sharing, and mercy. That's why, when you shake someone's hand, you do it with your right hand, the hand of sharing.

The left column is all about taking: the desire to receive for the self alone. I want and I want it now, and I don't care who I step on to get it.

The central column is the balance between taking and sharing. It's imperative that you create balance between the right column and left column. If you give too much, you will quickly get depleted. If you take too much, you will be despised.

You know those people who just give and give until they become exhausted, resentful, and bitter? They feel completely unappreciated because they gave so much and didn't receive anything in return. In our society, it is universally understood that it's good to give, but giving in an out-of-balance way that causes resentment is not good.

What can I say about takers? Stay the heck away from them. The UNIVERSAL WISDOM takes a very clear stand on this issue. It puts wicked people in the same category as selfish takers and teaches that, "wicked people are dead while they are still alive." (Babylonian Talmud, Brachot 18b)

Not that I'm an expert on zombies, but TV seems to do an accurate portrayal of them bashing through anything that stands in the way of them and their next feeding. Trust your intuition. If a person or situation feels unprincipled and/or morally bereft, it is usually so.

In order to manifest Light & Fulfillment here in the *Finite Realm*, you need to become a master at "taking so that you can share," (central column). This is the ultimate state of existence, as it keeps the **bridge** to the *Infinite Realm* open, sturdy, and able to funnel Light & Fulfillment to you whenever you need it.

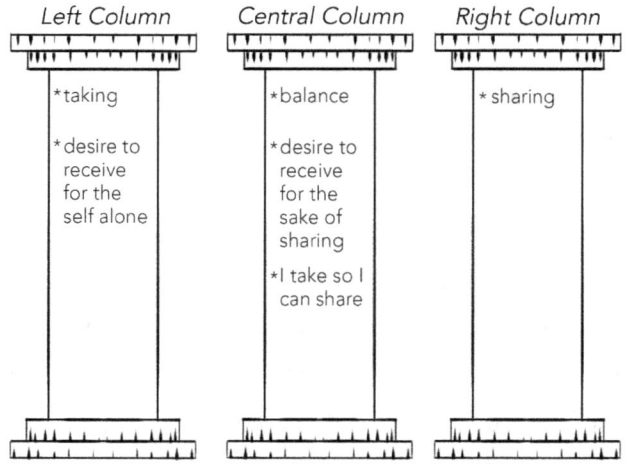

3-COLUMN SYSTEM
for manifesting Light & Fulfillment in the *Finite Realm*

Left Column	Central Column	Right Column
*taking	*balance	*sharing
*desire to receive for the self alone	*desire to receive for the sake of sharing	
	*I take so I can share	

The following examples will shed light on how to create this all-important central column:

EXAMPLE #1

You're starting a brand-new business. You start with the consciousness of, "I want to take as much as I can from everyone, rip them off, and give them an inferior product. There will be no return policy, and no one is getting his or her money back." This scenario falls under the left column, taking, in the **3-COLUMN SYSTEM** diagram.

or

You're starting a brand-new business. You're going to give your product away for free. You refuse to take money in return. This is an example of right-column thinking. What will eventually happen to the business? It will go under, of course, because you will give and give until you have nothing left. Giving without receiving is a recipe for disaster. So how do you create this balance between giving and receiving?

When you start any new endeavor, when people feel that you are there to serve them, share with them, care about them, the results will always be positive. If they feel, however, that you opened your business with the sole intent of taking money from them, they will stay away. The central column way is to always start with the right column, sharing, and then don't forget to access the left column, receiving. Otherwise, your new endeavor won't be able to survive. If you don't charge a fair price for your service/product, you won't be able to pay your bills and stay in business.

You <u>take</u> money so that you can <u>share</u> a product/service that will benefit people and make their lives better. You <u>take</u> so that you can <u>share</u>. That's called central column, balance.

EXAMPLE #2

You desperately need a vacation. You're a type A kind of person. You're wrung out and exhausted. You've been giving and giving to everyone: boss, kids, hubby, friends, community. All of a sudden, you snap and say, "I need a vacation and I'm going to dip into the kids' college fund to pay for it. I want a beach and lots of piña coladas and leave me alone." Notice the **language**, it's the **language** of the *Finite Realm*. Left column, <u>taking</u>.

or

"I've been working really hard. I'm really tired. I'm going on vacation. I'm going to rest and rejuvenate because when I come back, I'll be in a much better frame of mind so that I can give back to my family, give back to my community, and give back to my job" central column, I <u>take</u> so that I can <u>share</u>.

EXAMPLE #3

Parents falling into the trap of right column parenting: just giving and giving kids whatever they want. What does your relationship with those kids look like? Eventually, they become brats. They take from you. They expect from you. They don't willingly do anything for you and they don't respect you and they are selfish. Being a central-column parent is one of the greatest gifts you can give your children.

Let's say a child came to a parent and said, "I want a brand-new video game, and I want it *now*. All my friends have it." A central-column parent would say, "Really, that's great; I'm happy you know what you want, but what are you going to do to earn it?"

Remember BREAD OF SHAME? If you take without earning, you remain stuck in the *Finite Realm,* which makes it impossible to build **bridges** to the *Infinite Realm*. The child will take (left column) the video game, but how is he going to activate the right column, sharing? He has to do something to earn it. Central column cannot occur when BREAD OF SHAME is present. Trust me, you want to avoid being the cause of BREAD OF SHAME at all costs.

According to the UNIVERSAL WISDOM, the three columns are also represented as colors. The right column is white. Mother's milk is white, the ultimate in sharing. The left column is red. Red is the color of heat. When you get angry and reactive, you get red in the face; you see red. Red is the color of our taking and selfish nature. It represents our desire to receive for the self alone.

In Western culture, we don't often envision a person who is enlightened wearing red. They are usually surrounded in white light, wearing white angelic robes. It's no accident then, in Amsterdam, the free-lifestyle area is called the red-light district. Red is all about "I need, I want. I don't care about the consequences, me, me, me, without any restrictions." That's red; that's the *Finite Realm*.

We have red and white blood cells. What do the red blood cells do? They take (left column) oxygen. What do the white blood cells do? They fight to keep the body healthy. They are the immune system. They share (right column) with the whole body.

The central column is green, the color of balance. What balances the planet? The forests and the trees, all things green. They take CO2, carbon dioxide that suffocates and turns it into life-giving oxygen and food that nourishes the planet. Wherever you have more green, you have a more balanced atmosphere and the weather will be more temperate and balanced.

Again, the optimal state of existence is when you <u>take so that you can share</u>. Living a central-column way of life manifests as Light & Fulfillment in all areas of your life.

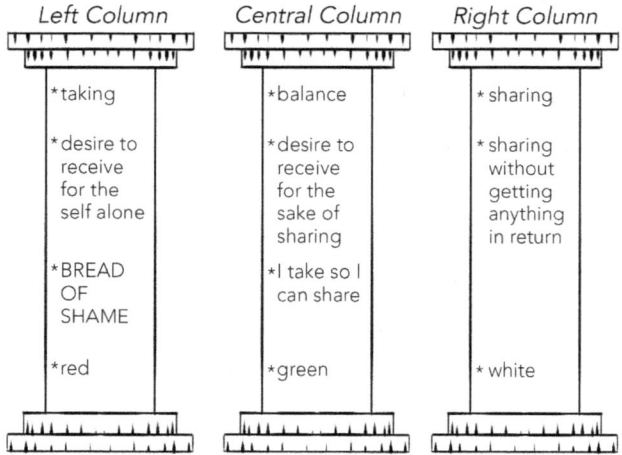

Astrology also has its place in the **3-COLUMN SYSTEM** for manifesting Light & Fulfillment. First, however, please note that the UNIVERSAL WISDOM uses astrology only as a tool to help us identify *tikune*, not something that defines our existence. We are not bound by the stars. We are meant to rise above the stars. Astrology is used to help us understand the nature of the Universe and our *tikune* (what we need to fix).

We all have three major influences: our natal sign, our rising sign, and our moon sign. With a composite of the three, you get a much better picture of what your *tikune* is. If you understand some basic astrology, you can understand shared human characteristics and use that information to know yourself and others better.

Each one of the signs has its negatives and positives. Also, each of the signs has its general *tikune*. This is the end of the discussion on astrology. It's not possible to do the topic justice at this juncture, so please forgive its exclusion at this time. The good news is that I have lectures on astrology that can be downloaded from my website.

The **3-COLUMN SYSTEM** and its great directive, <u>I take so that I can share</u>, is the last and final tool to **bridge** to the *Infinite Realm*.

Bridges to Light & Fulfillment

Bridge:

#1: Monitor your internal dialogue.

#2: I am a loving, caring, sharing creator.

#3: I made it happen; I am cause.

#4: 4-Step Creator Process.

#5: Do your *tikune*.

#6: I take so I can share.

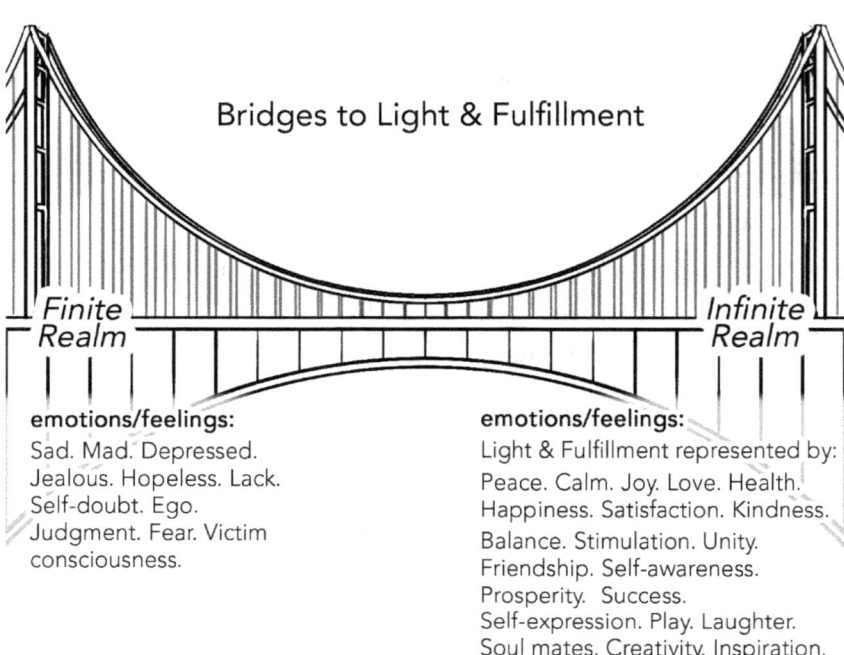

Bridges to Light & Fulfillment

Finite Realm

emotions/feelings:
Sad. Mad. Depressed. Jealous. Hopeless. Lack. Self-doubt. Ego. Judgment. Fear. Victim consciousness.

language:
I want...
I don't like...
I don't want...

body ruled by: <u>bad guy</u>
- five senses
- shrinking vessel
- effect
- BREAD OF SHAME
- reactive

Infinite Realm

emotions/feelings:
Light & Fulfillment represented by: Peace. Calm. Joy. Love. Health. Happiness. Satisfaction. Kindness. Balance. Stimulation. Unity. Friendship. Self-awareness. Prosperity. Success. Self-expression. Play. Laughter. Soul mates. Creativity. Inspiration. Tranquility. Wisdom. Pleasure. Clarity. Make a difference. To share. Purpose. To serve. Curiosity. Transformation. Excitement. Motivation. Exhilaration. Serenity. Adventure. Spirituality. Compassion. Connection to a Higher Power. Being in the moment. Family. Freedom. Enlightenment.

language:
I am a loving, caring, sharing creator.

soul ruled by: <u>GOOD GUY</u>
- intuition
- expanding soul
- cause
- creator
- proactive

The minute you decide to live in "I take so I can share" (central column), you never take on more than you can chew. The universe knows that you're committed to living a central column, balanced life, and it will fall in line to work with you.

Many times people will call and ask me to do them a favor: someone is sick and needs food, a lift to the doctor, someone to pick up their kids from school, etc. It always amazes me, when I do agree to share, even when I know I can't spare the time, usually five minutes later I get a call, "Don't worry; somebody else has already done the errand." Thank you, Universe!

There are amazing benefits to living a balanced life, but I must share this caveat with you. When you share, do not—and I repeat, *do not*—expect to receive something in return from the person who you shared with. You receive something greater than anything any human being can give to you. You gain access to the *Infinite Realm*, the home of Light & Fulfillment and the Higher Power.

We oftentimes think that if we give something away, our time, money, love, etc., that we are never going to get it back. WRONG!!! That's *Finite* thinking. When you take so that you can share (central column), you tap into the *Infinite Realm*. There is no lack there; there is no end there. There is just more and more of the good stuff. If you give more, you get more. You create a circuitry of giving and receiving that goes on and on.

Boundaries are very important in this process. If you can share and do so without resentment, do it. But the minute you feel resentment, don't do it. This is how you use **Bridge #3**: Monitor your inner dialogue. Once you identify that you feel resentment (step #1 of the **4-Step Creator Process**) the central column response is, "Thank you very much for the opportunity. I can't do it right now. But try me again another time."

Set your boundaries with grace. It's OK to say no. It's OK to say no to your children because you're doing them the greatest service, the greatest sharing, by teaching them how to do for themselves—to be the creator of their own lives and to be able to say, "Yes, I did it! I made it happen!"

But be on guard, because the <u>bad guy</u> will want to horn in on this. He will try to tell you to stop your sharing because there's not going to be anything left for you. Now, you are stronger and wiser; you know that isn't true. Give from your heart without resentment and without expecting anything from the people to whom you give. You can, however, expect to receive back from the Universe Light & Fulfillment, everything you want.

The UNIVERSAL WISDOM teaches that when it's time for you to go back "home" (please God, not until 120 years of age, in the greatest of health, wealth, wisdom, and fulfillment), the only thing that you can take with you, that follows you from lifetime to lifetime, are the hordes of guardian angels you created with the good deeds (*mitzvahs*) you did and the "**bridges**" you created. These guardian angels protect and guide you on this earthly plane and beyond. This is what you create when you live in the central column. This is the greatest reward of all.

When you live a balanced life (central column), <u>I take so I can share</u>, something miraculous happens. In addition to the Light & Fulfillment and guardian angels you receive, you also create a mantle of protection that follows you from lifetime to lifetime. The UNIVERSAL WISDOM teaches that you are always in the right place at the right time. You're always protected and you're always supported. How do I know this?

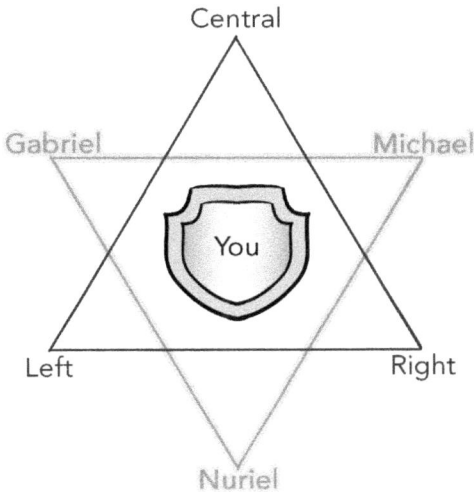

Magen David (Shield of David)

This diagram is typically referred to as the Jewish Star, but its Hebrew name, *"Magen David,"* means the Shield of David. The upper triangle represents the *Infinite Realm,* and is labeled right, left, and central (the upper triangle represents the metaphysical/*Infinite Realm* **3-COLUMN SYSTEM**).

The lower triangle represents the *Finite Realm*. And how do I know how to label it? *Magen* in Hebrew is spelled *mem, gimel, nun*. It is the acronym for three great angels: Michael, Gabriel, and Nuriel. The function of the archangels is to shield and protect humanity. When you live in the consciousness of I take so I can share (central column), it places you smack in the middle of this protective shield.

The Shield of David is neither a political nor religious symbol. It's a formula for achieving "light," fulfillment, and protection. Doesn't knowing this give you goose bumps? It does for me, no matter how many times I teach it. It's so awesome, comforting, and reassuring!

CHAPTER 15

Soul Pods

s we come to the end of the book, I want to leave you with a Universal Truth that will make your transformation into the best version of you a joyful, supportive, communal, and shared experience.

UNIVERSAL TRUTH #7
Surround yourself with like-minded people, as your level of consciousness will fall to the level of the lowest member of the group.

It is the rare person who can do this work alone. There is such power and truth in the statement that there is "strength in numbers." My mentor tells a story about how lions hunt. On the African Sahara, the lion picks as their prey the gazelles that stray from the herd. Choose your "herd" wisely; don't pick just any group. Align yourself with the people who share the same vision for a better life and world, and don't stray from this perception.

It's very important to turn to those supportive friends who can give you a reality check when you're in a heated moment or when you're straying away from the "herd." You want those people in your life, those who will gently—or sometimes not so gently—tell it the way it is. They aren't afraid to let you know when you're breaking **bridges** instead of building them.

I had a lady in a previous class say to me, "You know, as I have been learning and transforming, it has come to my attention that a lot of the people I know are not on this path with me, and it's causing me pain. I don't know what to do about it, I feel like I am losing some of my friends and family members."

I replied, "You're absolutely right. You're learning wisdom that is changing the way you look at the world. You want to be more positive. You want more from life. You want to be a creator. You don't want to listen to people whine and complain. You want to be a better, improved person, and typically, people want to take the easy way out or stay with the same old programming."

It's not easy to let go of people and relationships that no longer serve you. You can keep some and let go of others. You'll be able to strike a balance. The reality is, however, that there are people in your social circle who are not ready to do this work with you now. No one knows what the future holds, so your job is to stand firm in the *Infinite Realm* and to lead by example.

Don't preach to people who don't want to hear. Do surround yourself with people who are on a parallel journey, because when you need them, they'll be there to give you a much-needed reality check and the support you need to carry on.

Be very vigilant about whom you are hanging out with. If you're hanging around with a bunch of people who talk badly about others and judge everyone, you're going to find something to judge. This negativity is contagious.

Your level of consciousness will fall to the level of the lowest member of the group. Yes, we are all human, and, yes, it's so juicy and yummy to gossip, to be negative and judgmental. "Misery loves company." But the UNIVERSAL WISDOM warns about this: If you hang around with foolish people, you become foolish.

It's a sickness, so choose your friends wisely. Know that during those times when you feel that you can't build the "**bridge**" anymore, it's breaking and you need help, you will be able to get the support you need from your "soul pod" to continue your journey.

You must guard your "**bridges**"; post sentries on both ends, and do everything you can to stay in the *Infinite Realm*. Post a sign: "No negative people allowed." This is one of the greatest gifts you can give yourself.

CHAPTER 16

Thank You and Keep in Touch

Thank you so much for letting me manifest my life's purpose by sharing this ancient, immutable, tried-and-true UNIVERSAL WISDOM with you.

Now go and live yours!

If you're already doing so, great. If you are just beginning to discover your life's purpose, great. Wherever you are on this grand adventure, do it with more passion and excitement. Wake up each morning knowing that it's a new day and all good and wonderful things are possible.

Take comfort and strength from the knowledge that you are now armed with the tools to reveal Light & Fulfillment, everything humanity/your soul craves. Keep filling your spiritual tank. The best is yet to come.

Let's keep in touch. I want to hear about your "aha" moments, your successes with overcoming challenges, and how amazing it feels to have the "light" as your faithful companion.

There are numerous ways we can stay connected; add your name to my email list, friend me on Facebook, and join our online community. Contact me anytime to schedule a private coaching session or arrange a seminar in your workplace or community.

It has been an honor and a privilege, and if you will allow me:

I bless you with the power, strength, and perseverance to become a master bridge maker, strengthen your GOOD GUY, do your tikune/tikunim, and live your life's purpose. May you choose to overcome all your challenges with grace and dignity, thereby shortening them and infusing them with mercy. May your ongoing journey to the Infinite Realm be guided by a sure and driving desire to live a life of Light & Fulfillment. This is your destiny. Never give up. The Universal Light Force is your partner, and so am I.

With much love and gratitude,
    Anne Shoshana Deakter

ACKNOWLEDGMENTS

This book is dedicated to my beloved parents. They gave me life and educated me in the life skills necessary to make this book a reality. My father, of blessed memory, taught me to live my dreams and to see life as the greatest adventure of all. With much gratitude, I thank my mother for standing up for women's rights and empowerment and for always telling me that I can be anything I want to be.

My treasured partner in life is the Universal Light Force. I thank the Higher Power for creating the space and opportunities for me to express the God-given talents I was born with and the ability to recognize them and use them for creating good in the world.

Thank you to the many people who've made the sharing of this *infinite*ly important UNIVERSAL WISDOM possible. I have been blessed with amazing mentors, teachers, students, friends, and family members who have tirelessly encouraged me to birth this book into the world.

My husband, Daniel, has been a rock and a constant source of support. Thank you for believing in me and keeping the vision alive, especially during the times when I lost my way and couldn't see. My sons, Zev and Michael, you inspire me to keep working on myself, to be the best I can be.

The passion, loving hearts, knowledge, and caring of Rabbi Shaul Youdkevitch and his wife, Osnat, have made it possible to reveal this much-needed healing wisdom now. Thank you for sharing my life, the ups and the downs, the bitter and the sweet. I look forward to sharing with you the miracles and wonders that are yet to come.

My holy brother, Rabbi Yehudah Greenberg, you have believed in me from day one. When I doubted myself, you lent me your heavenly eyes through which I got to see glimpses of the exalted "light." Your strength and belief that all is good and all will be good gives me the courage to keep blazing new trails.

I thank my mentor and coach, Dee Hilliard, for her insight, intuition, integrity, and unwavering belief and connection to the "light." You are a deep and endless source of love, inspiration, and support. Your ability to put into words the ways of the "light" is a gift beyond measure.

It is with great appreciation and respect that I thank Rabbi Efrem Goldberg, Senior Rabbi of Boca Raton Synagogue, and Rabbi Josh Broide, Outreach Rabbi of Boca Raton Synagogue. Having your support and teaching in the community has afforded me the opportunity to positively impact so many lives. It is an honor and a privilege to partner with you in doing the work of "tikune olam."

Thank you to Rabbi Moshe Schatz for his contribution in providing biblical sources, guidance and encouragement. Rabbi

Schatz is a Torah Scholar, Teacher and author of *Sparks of the Hidden Light*.

Thank you to my students and private clients for pushing me to write this book. You wanted something tangible to sink your teeth into. It was your constant nagging (ha-ha!) that made it all happen. Keep at me; I am open to receive the next "light"-revealing project that we can create together.

And finally, thank you to Michael Levin of BusinessGhost. You and your team turned a dream into a reality with grace and ease.

ABOUT THE AUTHOR

Born and raised in Montréal, Canada, Anne Shoshana Deakter received her BA in sociology and business and then moved to South Florida in her early twenties. Like many young adults, she did not know what her life's purpose was. She had an inkling that she liked working with and teaching people, so she got her second degree in teaching and continued on to pursue extensive graduate work at Florida Atlantic University's department of educational leadership and research methodology. Often it takes a "wake-up" call for most of us to make serious changes in our lives. Anne Shoshana's was the early death of her beloved father, and becoming a divorced single mom. Always the "seeker," she started looking for answers by learning multiple spiritual disciplines, including Kabbalah. For over two decades, Anne Shoshana has been a student and teacher of the ancient, immutable wisdom of the Old Testament, Mussar, and Kabbalah. She shares her journey and lives to inspire all who are ready to grow their next level of innovation. She has created a program where she fuses this Universal Wisdom with her experience as a leadership educator, life coach, and spiritual mentor to provide you with user-friendly tools. Why? So that you too, can go from *good* to *better*.

CONNECT WITH ANNE SHOSHANA DEAKTER

For more information on Anne Shoshana Deakter and her work, please reference the following:

Email: anneshoshanaD@gmail.com

Facebook: Anne Shoshana Deakter

Website: www.anneshoshanadeakter.com

www.ingramcontent.com/pod-product-compliance
Lightning Source LLC
Chambersburg PA
CBHW052058110526
44591CB00013B/2258